Sunset

Roses

by Hazel White and the Editors of Sunset Books

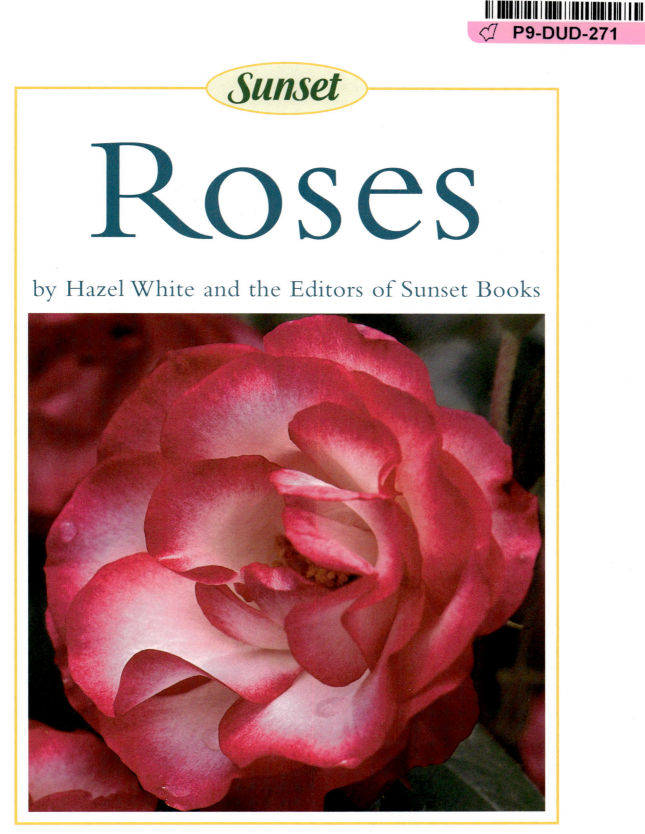

Menlo Park, California

A Message from the American Rose Society

The American Rose Society is proud to endorse Sunset Publishing's newest book on roses and rose care. Like all ARS-endorsed products, this publication has been thoroughly read, edited, and approved by expert "rosarians" from all around the country.

Founded more than 110 years ago, the American Rose Society is a nonprofit educational organization dedicated to the promotion, culture, and appreciation of the rose—America's national floral emblem.

I invite you to increase your appreciation of roses through the American Rose Society. Call 1-800-ROSE-911 or visit *www.ars.org* for more information about the programs and benefits of membership in the largest society in America dedicated to the world's favorite flower . . . and take time to smell your beautiful roses!

Michael C. Kromer

Michael C. Kromer
Executive Director, American Rose Society

PHOTOGRAPHERS

b = bottom; l = left; m = middle; r = right; t = top

Syl Arena: 3 b, 72, 75 br, 78 bl, 78 bmr, 80 bmr, 81 tl, 91 tm, 94 tl, 94 bml, 95 bl, 96 tl, 101 bml, 103 tl, 103 bl, 104 tm, 104 br, 109 tr, 111 bl, 113 tl, 126; **Scott Atkinson:** 45 ml, 45 bl, 45 br, 84 br, 85 bl, 107 tr, 112 bmr; **Marion Brenner:** 27; **Patricia J. Bruno/Positive Images:** 9 tr, 12 tr; **Gay Bumgarner/Positive Images:** 15 br; **Karen Bussolini:** 3 t, 4, 9 tl, 16 tr, 55 m, 58 bl, 61, 62, 87 bl; **Karen Bussolini/Positive Images:** 27 b; **R. S. Byther:** 46 mr; **Rob Cardillo:** 55 l, 78 tl, 80 tl, 82 tmr, 89 tr, 92 bm, 93 tm, 98 tl, 106 tml, 106 bl, 107 t, 108 br, 113 br; **David Cavagnaro:** 17 t; **Van Chaplin:** 21 tr; **The Conrad-Pyle Co.:** 110 br; **Ken Conway:** 47 bl; **Eric Crichton/The Garden Picture Library:** 11 b; **Claire Curran:** 1, 45 tr, 75 tmr, 76 tr, 81 br, 83 br, 84 tm, 91 tl, 92 bl, 95 bm, 100 tl, 109 bl, 112 tl, 122; **Robin B. Cushman:** 18 l, 77 bml, 81 tml, 81 tl, 82 bml, 88 bml, 99 br; **R. Todd Davis:** 85 ml, 98 bl, 112 tr, 123; **Alan and Linda Detrick:** 24, 30, 46 br, 47 r, 58 br, 80 tr, 116 tr, 116 tm, 117 br; **Andrew Drake:** 76 bl, 124; **Ken Druse:** 111 tl, 111 tr; **Philip Edinger:** 102 tmr, 105 tm; **Derek Fell:** 78 tr, 117 bl, 118 br; **Roger Foley:** 14 l inset, 15 t, 67; **Steven Gunther:** 10 br; **Lynne Harrison:** 6 tl, 82 bl, 89 tml, 101 br, 105 bl, 106 tl, 110 tmr, 110 tr; **Heirloom Roses, Inc.:** 102 bl, 118 tl; **Saxon Holt:** 8 l inset, 14 tr, 17 b, 19 t, 55 r, 58 tr, 63, 71, 74 bm, 81 tmr, 83 tm, 89 br, 90 bml, 92 br, 93 br, 94 bmr, 94 br, 95 tl, 96 bl, 97 tm, 100 bml, 101 bl, 101 bmr, 102 bm, 102 br, 103 tr, 104 bm, 107 tm, 107 bm, 108 bl, 108 bmr, 115 tl, 115 tm, 117 tr, 118 tml, 119 br, 121, 128; **Jerry Howard/Positive Images:** 20 tr; **Jackson & Perkins:** 118 bl, 125 tr; **Dency Kane:** 18 l inset, 58 tl, 87 tml, 87 bmr, 88 tr, 88 bmr, 92 tm, back cover r; **Kathryn Kleinman:** 6 br, 74 bl, 108 bml; **Janet Loughrey:** 3 upper m, 10 bl, 20 br, 22, 75 tml, 75 bm, 79 bl, 80 bl, 86 m, 86 r, 87 tr, 89 bm, 90 bl, 91 tr, 91 br, 94 tr, 94 bl, 95 tr, 95 br, 98 br, 99 tl, 106 br, 109 bm, 112 bml, 112 br, 113 bm, 117 tl, back cover tl; **Charles Mann:** 9 br, 16 tl, 17 b inset, 28 tl, 105 bm; **Ells Marugg:** 114 bm, 118 bmr; **Mayer/Le Scanff/The Garden Picture Library:** 10 tl; **David McDonald/Photo Garden:** 19 bl, 76 tl, 86 l, 87 bml, 109 br; **Andrew McKinney:** 45 tl, 94 tmr; **Nor'East Mini Roses:** 114 bl, 118 tmr, 118 tr, 120 br; **Jerry Pavia:** 6 tmr, 8 l, 13 t, 14 l, 15 bl, 16 b, 18 tr, 19 ml, 28 tr, 28 br, 38, 53, 75 tr, 75 bl, 76 tm, 76 bmr, 77 br, 78 bml, 79 tm, 79 tr, 80 br, 82 tl, 82 tr, 82 bmr, 83 tl, 83 tr, 83 bl, 85 tl, 88 tm, 89 tmr, 96 tm, 96 bmr, 96 br, 97 tr, 97 br, 100 bl, 100 bmr, 103 bl, 105 tr, 105 br, 106 tmr, 109 tl, 110 tml, 112 bl, 115 tr, 115 br, 116 bl, 116 bm, 116 br, 117 tml, 118 bml, 120 bl, 125 bl, back cover bl; **Pamela Peirce:** 48; **Ben Phillips/Positive Images:** 79 br; **Norman A. Plate:** 8 tr, 36, 59, 69, 77 tl, 95 tm, 98 tm, 114 br; **Howard Rice/The Garden Picture Library:** 12 tl; **Susan A. Roth:** 3 lower m, 6 bm, 9 bl, 10 tr, 19 mr, 20 mr, 56, 74 tr, 75 tl, 77 tr, 77 bl, 78 tmr, 79 tl, 80 tml, 80 tmr, 81 bl, 82 tml, 82 br, 84 bl, 84 bml, 85 tl, 87 tl, 87 tmr, 88 br, 89 tl, 90 tr, 90 br, 92 tl, 92 tr, 93 tl, 93 bl, 94 tml, 96 tr, 96 bml, 97 tl, 98 tr, 98 bm, 99 tm, 99 tr, 99 bl, 100 br, 101 t, 102 tml, 103 tml, 105 tl, 106 tr, 107 bl, 107 br, 108 t, 109 tm, 110 tl, 110 bl, 111 tmr, 112 tm, 113 bl, 119 tl, 120 bm; **Kjell Sandved/Visuals Unlimited:** 46 tr; **Richard Shiell:** 6 tl, 19 br, 76 bml, 78 br, 84 tr, 84 bmr, 85 bm, 85 br, 90 tl, 91 bl, 102 tl, 103 tmr, 104 tl, 114 t, 116 tl, 117 bm, 119 tm, 120 tr; **Southern Progress Corp.:** 13 bl; **Anthony Tesselaar:** 90 bmr; **Michael S. Thompson:** 6 bl, 6 bmr, 20 l, 21 ml, 54, 70, 78 tml, 87 br, 88 tl, 89 bl, 93 tr, 97 bl, 100 tm, 100 tr, 102 tr, 104 tr, 104 bl, 106 bmr, 111 tml, 111 br, 113 tr, 115 bl, 117 tmr, 119 tr, 119 bl, 120 tl, 120 tm, 127; **Mark Turner:** 17 m, 28 bl, 46 tl, 46 bl, 65, 76 br, 84 tl, 88 bl, 91 bm; **Juliette Wade/The Garden Picture Library:** 12 b; **Ron West:** 47 tl; **judywhite/GardenPhotos.com:** 11 t, 13 br, 21 tl, 21 br, 47 tr, 106 bml, 111 bm; **Lee Anne White:** 21 bl; **Tom Wyatt:** 74 br, 80 bl, 115 bm.

Acknowledgments

Special thanks to the six regional consultants—Russ Bowermaster, Kathleen Brenzel, Larry Parton, Michael Ruggiero, Peter Schneider, and Peggy Van Allen (see page 121)—who gave us lists of their favorite roses, from which we wrote chapter 4, and to the American Rose Society for its help with the manuscript.

SUNSET BOOKS

Vice President, General Manager:
  Richard A. Smeby
Vice President, Editorial Director:
  Bob Doyle
Production Director: Lory Day
Director of Operations:
  Rosann Sutherland
Sales Development Director: Linda Barker
Art Director: Vasken Guiragossian

STAFF FOR THIS BOOK

Managing Editor and Copy Editor:
  Zipporah W. Collins
Writer: Hazel White
Sunset Books Senior Editor:
  Marianne Lipanovich
Photography Editor: Cynthia Del Fava
Production Coordinator: Danielle Javier
Proofreaders: Desne Ahlers, Mu'afrida Bell
Indexer: Andrew Joron
Computer Production: Joan Olson
Illustrator: Erin O'Toole

10 9 8 7 6 5
First printing January 2003

Cover photos by Claire Curran: *center,* 'Caribbean' (see page 75); *border,* roses for cutting.

For additional copies of *Roses* or any other Sunset book, call 1-800-526-5111 or visit us at *www.sunsetbooks.com*

contents

CHAPTER ONE

Placing Roses in the Garden

A ROSE IS A ROSE? NOT REALLY. The "queen of flowers" has many guises. She doesn't only stand aloof and regal behind clipped boxwood hedges in rose beds cut into the lawn. She also holds her own in the back of the border with the brawniest flowering shrubs; scales walls and even the roof; forms a chorus line along a garden boundary; swings around pyramids and posts; jazzes up pots with bold companions; and spills innocently over the path like a soft perennial. ❧ *In this chapter, you'll see just how many places a rose can grow. On the practical side, you need a place that's the right size for the particular rose. Beyond that, it's a matter of playing with the aesthetic possibilities of a rose's color, flower form, and fragrance. Don't overlook the beauty of fall hips and changing foliage color. And keep in mind that under the prettiness, or voluptuousness, may lurk some beautiful thorns.*

'Penelope' (page 96) makes a fine hedge at the Antique Rose Emporium in Texas.

Getting to Know Roses

There are more than twelve thousand varieties of roses for sale in the world. Next time you stop to smell a few in a rose garden, take a look at the details of the blossoms and how the types of roses are placed.

FULL: *'Yves Piaget'*.

LOOKING AT THE BLOSSOMS

A detailed examination of rose blossoms reveals differences not just in color but also in petal count, petal shape, flower shape (when viewed from the side), and the way the blossoms are carried on the plant. The huge variety in the combination of these characteristics is one reason why roses are so adored.

SINGLE A single rose has 11 or fewer petals. *Rosa eglanteria* is a single rose. Its blossoms are flat in shape; they are usually borne in a small cluster, but sometimes they appear singly.

SINGLE: Rosa eglanteria.

SEMIDOUBLE A semidouble rose has between 12 and 16 petals. 'Delicata' is a semidouble rose. Its petals are ruffled; the blossoms are cupped in shape, and they appear in clusters.

DOUBLE A double rose has between 17 and 25 petals. 'Pascali' is a double rose. Its blossoms have a high center, typical of hybrid tea roses, and reflexed outer petals (they curve down). 'Abbaye de Cluny' blooms are deeply cupped in shape and borne singly on the bush.

FULL A full rose has between 26 and 40 petals. 'Yves Piaget' has full blossoms. The petals have a wavy edge; the blossoms are deeply cupped, almost globular, in shape, and they appear singly.

VERY FULL A very full rose has 41 petals or more. 'The Pilgrim' has 170 petals; it has a rosette

VERY FULL: *'The Pilgrim'* (above), *'Mme. Hardy'* (below).

shape (many short petals, with a flat, low center), and its inner petals are "quartered" (folded into four distinct sections rather than around a cone). The very full blossoms of 'Mme. Hardy' are cupped when young but flatten as they age; the petals surround a green eye, or pip.

SEMIDOUBLE: *'Delicata'*.

DOUBLE: *'Pascali'* (left), *'Abbaye de Cluny'* (right).

LOOKING AT THE PLANTS

Rose bushes are natural choices for flower beds and shrub borders; some also make fine hedges or container plants. The largest are the old garden roses, grandifloras, and shrub roses. Hybrid teas and floribundas generally grow with more restraint. Miniature roses are the smallest; some reach only 1 foot tall. For a little formality, consider a standard rose, a bush rose grown on a tall bare stem; a patio rose is a small standard.

Climbing roses grow on vertical surfaces or free-standing supports. The most vigorous ones, the ramblers, will cover a house roof or grow to the top of a large tree. More moderate climbers clothe arbors and tall walls. Small climbers, sometimes called pillar roses, are suitable for a pyramid or trellis. In addition to the roses that are classified as climbers, there are old garden roses and shrub roses that climb, and climbing miniature roses.

Ground cover roses make a low, mounding carpet of color up to 8 feet wide. They are most often massed on a slope or an area of the garden where other knee-high shrubs might be used. They also make good container plants. Look for them in the landscape roses section, pages 86–100.

More details about the characteristics of each rose type appear in chapter 4, "More than 390 Recommended Roses," on pages 73–120.

OLD GARDEN ROSE

RAMBLER

CLIMBER

SHRUB

GRANDIFLORA

HYBRID TEA

FLORIBUNDA

PILLAR

STANDARD

MINIATURES

GROUND COVERS

Small Gardens

Small gardens are often the most beautiful. Save space by raising your roses off the ground (see pages 14–15). Use miniature roses, grow roses in pots—there are many options in small spaces.

ABOVE: *Catmint (Nepeta) and pink and coral diascias make perfect pot companions for 'Sunset Celebration' (page 84). They tolerate the rose's regular irrigation and feeding, but they don't compete for them. Visually, the diascias play off the pretty pinks and apricots in the rose, and the cool catmint blue makes those warm colors even warmer.*

LEFT: *Light and cool colors recede, creating a sense of space, which is particularly useful in small areas. Yet white, the coolest color of all, isn't a background color, quite the contrary; it's fresh and bright and attracts the eye faster than red or orange. This white garden is composed of an 'Iceberg' rose (page 92), 'White Nancy' lamium, white Silene uniflora, and foliage plants with white-variegated leaves.*

INSET: *The multiple colors in some roses, such as this miniature 'Rainbow's End' (page 119), can help unify the elements in a garden. Here, from late spring until frost, the house and the plantings have become an eye-catching composition of pastel and hot pinks and yellows.*

ABOVE: *Pots of roses—shrubby or trailing, alone or in a line or mixed with pots of other plants—can make a bold statement on steps, pillars, along the tops of walls, or on the floor of a balcony or deck. Keep potted roses well watered and fertilized (see pages 39 and 41).*

Recommended for Containers

Miniature roses are obvious candidates for container plantings. But polyanthas, floribundas, and even shrub and old garden roses can also work successfully provided they are compact. The list below includes all types.

PINK ROSES

China Doll, p. 89
Cupcake, p. 115
Flower Carpet, p. 90
Rose de Rescht, p. 107
Sexy Rexy, p. 98
The Fairy, p. 100

YELLOW ROSES

Baby Love, p. 114

WHITE ROSES

French Lace, p. 91
Gourmet Popcorn, p. 116
Sea Foam, p. 98

OTHER ROSES

Marie Curie, p. 94
Regensburg, p. 97

LEFT: *'Hawkeye Belle', 'Wind Chimes', and 'Mme. Isaac Pereire' (page 104) weave along the fence, 'Sombreuil' (page 113) climbs the house wall, and 'Zéphirine Drouhin' (page 107) spills over the stair rail. They help to screen this little space, and their beauty and perfume storm the senses of everyone entering here. Design: Paula Manchester.*

ABOVE: *Because they are relatively small, miniature roses often get lost in mixed plantings. But here their delicacy is beautifully displayed among the contrasting shapes and colors of Japanese blood grass* (Imperata), *blue elymus grass, and iris.*

Cottage Gardens

Although they look haphazard and easy, successful cottage gardens result from careful planning and usually many experiments. If you need more ideas for introducing some visual order into a chaotic planting, turn to pages 12–13.

ABOVE: *In a cottage garden, plants tumble over and thread through one another. Two or more different climbing roses might romp together over an arch. Here, a 'Victoria' clematis twines itself around a 'William Baffin' rose (page 113). Design: Paula and Peter Manchester.*

LEFT: *A cool flower border of fragrant 'Iceberg' roses (page 92), catmint (Nepeta), and a species geranium is arranged with the tallest plant at the back and the smallest in the front. This layering creates an illusion of depth in a narrow bed.*

BOTTOM LEFT: *Planting climbing roses among the species geraniums, euphorbias, and stachys makes it possible to maintain a sense of fullness and depth to this flower border as it narrows at the steps. Pale and cool colors recede into the distance; the garden would seem shorter if the roses were red. Design: Margaret de Haas van Dorsser.*

BOTTOM RIGHT: *A successful cottage garden gives an impression of profusion and pleasing chaos. A glimpse of a contrasting firm line— a fence or an arbor post—accentuates the "wildness."*

LEFT: *Seemingly a riot of color, this garden succeeds because the colors are of a similar intensity. Mixing pastel flowers among the orange climbing 'Warm Welcome' rose (page 120), the blue Himalayan poppy (Meconopsis), and the chartreuse euphorbia would tip the composition into an irritating jumble of colors.*

BELOW: *In this double garden border, the colors are hot and visually striking but also harmonious. The harmony derives from a restrained use of color—shades of red, pink, and yellow, with a little contrasting blue and fresh white as accents. Repeating the pink and red roses, astilbe, and lychnis along the borders also contributes to the sense of order and quietness.*

Recommended Companion Plants

Most roses need generous amounts of fertilizer and water, so choose companion plants that have similar needs. Don't crowd your roses; plant companions at least 1½ feet away. Here are some of the best choices:

Artemisia 'Powis Castle'
Delphinium elatum, English delphinium
Gypsophila paniculata, baby's breath
Hemerocallis, daylily
Iris, especially Siberian iris
Lavandula angustifolia 'Hidcote' and 'Munstead', English lavender
Myosotis, forget-me-not
Nemesia
Nepeta × *faassenii,* catmint
Penstemon × *gloxinioides,* border penstemon

Formal Gardens

Repetition, symmetry, geometric lines and patterns, clipped hedges or topiary, an axis with a focal point: these formal elements lend grace and elegance to a rose garden.

LEFT: *Formal in its simplicity— brilliant red 'Trumpeter' floribunda roses, an emerald carpet of lawn, a dark, clipped hedge—this garden blooms from late spring into fall and is always a place of peace.*

RIGHT: *Reducing the variety of textures, colors, and shapes within a garden vignette allows garden guests to take in the details better. Note how the shape of the wall finial mimics the line of the clipped conifer and the curves of the rose buds.*

Boxwood (Buxus) hedges traditionally edge formal rose beds to hide the roses' bare ankles, but these bushy roses have plenty of low foliage of their own. The raised urn is a traditional focal point for the end of a garden axis.

ABOVE: *Because of the repetition of the pillars, a pergola looks more formal than an arch or an arbor. Here a balance between formal and informal has been established: the stucco columns tend toward the formal, but the variety in rose colors and the absence of a focal point or clipped shrubs undercut the formality. Design: Jack Chandler Associates.*

In this rose garden, in Birmingham, Alabama, the fountain directs the eye to a wall ornament between a pair of lattice arches. Aligning the elements like this to create a strong sight line is one way to establish a sense of formality. Design: Norman Kent Johnson.

'Gertrude Jekyll', a large shrub rose, contributes antique charm and heady perfume to this Islamic knot garden ribboned with barberry (Berberis). To keep the rose low-growing and the pattern of the garden clear, the canes must be pegged (see pages 70–71).

pages 70–71

Recommended for Beautiful Form

Traditionally, formal rose gardens are planted with hybrid tea roses, the roses with the most elegant blossoms. Their long, slender buds slowly spiral open around a high center, making a tall triangle when you look at one from the side. The hybrid teas listed here have exquisite form.

PINK ROSES

Bride's Dream, p. 75
Classic Touch, p. 75
Tiffany, p. 84

RED ROSES

Dublin, p. 76
Ingrid Bergman, p. 78
Opening Night, p. 81
Uncle Joe, p. 85

YELLOW ROSES

Elina, p. 77

WHITE ROSES

Jardins de Bagatelle, p. 79
Moonstone, p. 80
Sheer Bliss, p. 83

OTHERS

Fragrant Cloud, p. 77
Gemini, p. 77
Sunset Celebration, p. 84
Touch of Class, p. 85
Vanilla Perfume, p. 85

Vertical Roses

Growing some roses vertically adds a third dimension of space to a garden and makes room for more plants below. It also brings the blossoms closer to eye level.

ABOVE: *'Cl. Cécile Brünner' (page 109) has a sweet rustic charm. From its small, beautifully formed, delicately fragrant, pink blossoms you'd never guess it is vigorous. Unless kept in check, it will climb off this fence and up into the neighboring trees. Design: Michael Bates.*

BELOW: *People can't help but pause on their way under this arch, clothed with the large-flowered climber 'America' (page 108). Each of its abundant flowers is a beautifully formed cup stuffed with petals; the blossoms appear all summer, and they are heavily perfumed.*

This pergola (a series of arches joined together) is purposefully missing a few beams. It's at the edge of a garden, where formality is giving way to nature and the process of time. The low wall offers a casual place to put up your feet and watch the sweetly scented white petals of 'Sombreuil', left (page 113), drift off in the breeze. Design: Jack Chandler Associates.

BELOW: *Upright roses with limber canes, like this 'Mme. Grégoire Staechelin', make fine climbers. They are easy to train, and the blossoms naturally sag through an arbor so you can get close to them. Climbing roses with a stiff habit, such as some sports of hybrid teas, tend to produce their blossoms high in the air if left to their own devices.*

Recommended Small Climbers

Climbing roses come in different sizes. Use rampant ones to cover large arbors or an unsightly shed. For small situations, grow modest climbers, such as the following:

PINK ROSES

Clair Matin, p. 109
Jeanne Lajoie, p. 117
Zéphirine Drouhin, p. 107

RED ROSES

Blaze, p. 108

WHITE ROSES

Sombreuil, p. 113

OTHERS

Fourth of July, p. 110
Garden Sun, p. 110
Handel, p. 111
Polka, p. 112
Shadow Dancer, p. 112
Warm Welcome, p. 120

LEFT: *'Dortmund' (page 110) decorates a blue pillar with a mauve finial in this garden of strong bright colors in Sagaponack, New York. Like many of the roses commonly described as pillar roses (or pillar-climbers), it can be just as easily used as a shrub. Design: Robert Dash.*

ABOVE: *This double red rose has just the right amount of elegance for this boundary fence. A single "wild" rose might look too rustic in relation to the house; a pale rose wouldn't attract attention; a multicolored rose might seem gaudy.*

Hedges and Ground Covers

New series of roses have been bred specifically for hedges and ground covers. They are designed to be low-maintenance, which is essential for mass plantings. Some older roses fit the bill, too.

Recommended for Hedges

For a tall hedge, 5 feet or higher, choose shrub roses or tall floribundas, and plant them about 3 feet apart. For a lower hedge, choose compact shrub roses or floribundas, and plant them about 1½ feet apart. Hybrid teas are generally too upright and bare at the base to make a good bushy hedge; if you use them, prune the canes to different heights so the leaves and flowers aren't all at the top. For a very low hedge, under 2½ feet tall, choose miniature roses (pages 114–120).

PINK ROSES

Bonica, p. 88
Conrad Ferdinand Meyer, p. 89
Pink Meidiland, p. 96
Simplicity, p. 98

RED ROSES

Hansa, p. 92
Knock Out, p. 93
Linda Campbell, p. 93
Robusta, p. 97

WHITE ROSES

Iceberg, p. 92
Sally Holmes, p. 97

OTHERS

Carefree Delight, p. 88
Carefree Wonder, p. 89
Escapade, p. 89

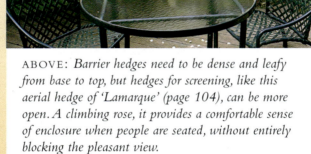

ABOVE: *Barrier hedges need to be dense and leafy from base to top, but hedges for screening, like this aerial hedge of 'Lamarque' (page 104), can be more open. A climbing rose, it provides a comfortable sense of enclosure when people are seated, without entirely blocking the pleasant view.*

ABOVE: Rosa rugosa *roses, the species (page 106) and the many hybrids (pages 86–100), make magnificent hedges. They are dense and leafy, disease resistant, and thorny (so impenetrable). They bloom over a long period, are fragrant, and produce beautiful tomato-shaped hips (see page 21) in summer and fall. Choose carefully: the species rose can grow 7 feet tall and wide, while 'Snow Owl' (page 99) stays about 3 feet by 3 feet. Design: Natureworks.*

BELOW: *Ground cover roses cover up the bare knobby ankles of this chorus line of 'Summer Fashion' standard roses. Use them in the same way in front of a climbing rose or hybrid tea roses that are bare at the base. If you choose a rose with thorns, be diligent about clearing the soil of weeds before you plant.*

LEFT: *'Iceberg' (page 92) (above) and pink 'Bonica' (page 88) (below) are two popular hedging choices. Both generally grow from 3 to 5 feet tall, but be aware that size depends very much on climate and growing conditions: 'Iceberg' can grow to 8 feet tall and wide in mild climates if it's well tended. 'Bonica' also makes a fine ground cover.*

BELOW: *'Flower Carpet' (page 90) produces a stunning display of blossoms all summer long in this perennials garden. Its companions are stachys, catmint (Nepeta), Artemisia 'Powis Castle', phormium, and daylilies (Hemerocallis). Design: Freeland Tanner.*

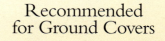

Recommended for Ground Covers

Ground cover roses arch or creep over the ground. They have dense foliage, are vigorous, and flower freely—some bloom nonstop until frost nips them. Plant the small shrubby types 2 feet apart; for large sprawling varieties, leave up to 5 feet between plants.

PINK ROSES

Flower Carpet, p. 90
Pink Meidiland, p. 96

RED ROSES

Gourmet Pheasant, p. 117
Red Cascade, p. 119
Red Ribbons, p. 97
Scarlet Meidiland, p. 97

YELLOW ROSES

Sun Runner, p. 99

WHITE ROSES

Sea Foam, p. 98
White Meidiland, p. 100

INSET: *Gardeners used to plant vigorous, lax ramblers, Bourbons, and hybrid perpetuals to cover large areas of ground. This rambler, Rosa banksiae 'Lutea' (page 105), could cover the entire bank if allowed.*

Fragrance

Fragrance is as important as color to most gardeners selecting roses. Place a fragrant rose where people have a chance to catch its perfume, and keep it well watered, which will help the petals excrete those micro-droplets of scent.

ABOVE: *An opulently perfumed, naturally arching old garden rose, like this 'Ispahan' damask, is beautiful to come upon at the edge of the garden. 'Ispahan' blooms for up to 2 months in early summer. Damask roses are grown commercially in central Europe for the production of attar of roses.*

LEFT: *The scent of these welcoming blooms of 'Golden Showers' (page 111), like that of several other roses, varies. To some, it is a very sweet perfume; others report no fragrance. One rose bush may produce more fragrance than another of the same variety; people's experience of scent differs; and blossoms may smell strongly in the morning but not at all by afternoon.*

INSET: *A sweet scent can lead you on a memorable journey through even a very small garden. The fruity fragrance of the 'New Dawn' rose (page 112) may bring you close enough to notice the interesting form of the* Clematis florida sieboldii *blossoms—and then to study the way the color changes on the blossoms of both plants as they age.*

LEFT: *To enjoy the fragrance of roses, you need to be close to the petals. This easily moved, comfortable wicker chair invites you to enjoy the strong sweet scent of the nodding blossoms of 'La Ville de Bruxelles' (page 103). Design: Michael Bates.*

If you have a good nose, you can learn to tell the difference between myriad rose fragrances.
CLOCKWISE FROM TOP LEFT: *'Queen Elizabeth' (page 82) smells slightly of moss and ferns, 'Jardins de Bagatelle' (page 79) smells of classic old-world rose, 'Dublin' (page 76) smells of raspberry, 'Belle Story' (page 87) smells of anise or myrrh.*

Recommended for Fragrance

Until fairly recently, perfume was most often associated with old garden roses. Now, to meet demand, new English (David Austin), Generosa, and Romantica varieties often have bountiful fragrance. The following list contains old and new highly scented roses, plus hybrid teas, a group usually lacking much scent. Roses with an asterisk (★) have won the James Alexander Gamble Fragrance Medal from the American Rose Society, for top-performing, intensely fragrant roses.

PINK ROSES

Conrad Ferdinand Meyer, p. 89
Crested Moss, p. 102
Dainty Bess, p. 76
Magna Charta, p. 105
Mme. Isaac Pereire, p. 104
Sarah Van Fleet, p. 98
★Tiffany, p. 84

RED ROSES

★Chrysler Imperial, p. 75
★Crimson Glory, p. 75
Dupuy Jamain, p. 102
Mister Lincoln, p. 80

YELLOW ROSES

★Sunsprite, p. 99

WHITE ROSES

Jardins de Bagatelle, p. 79
Kiftsgate, p. 111
Sheer Bliss, p. 83

OTHERS

Abraham Darby, p. 86
★Double Delight, p. 76
★Fragrant Cloud, p. 77
Intrigue, p. 93

Foliage, Thorns, Hips, and History

Many roses produce not only silky, scented blooms but also magnificent hips and leaves. Others are worth adding to the garden because of their monstrously large thorns—or because they are North American natives.

Decorative mossy glands on the sepals around the flower buds give moss roses their name. The moss feels soft on the centifolia mosses (such as 'Crested Moss', page 102, and 'William Lobb', page 107) and prickly on the damask mosses (such as 'Henri Martin', page 103). It sometimes has a pine scent.

ABOVE: *Rose hips come in many colors, sizes, and shapes—round and oblong, but also curved like flagons and bulging like tomatoes. Some are thick and waxy, some almost translucent.* TOP TO BOTTOM: *Hips of* Rosa rugosa *(page 106),* R. moyesii *(page 106), and* R. eglanteria *(page 105).*

ABOVE, LEFT: *The Green rose (Rosa chinensis viridiflora; page 103) doesn't flower like most roses; its sepals have taken the place of petals. Flower arrangers grow it for its novel green "blossoms," which appear all summer long.* RIGHT: *Curious prickles, reminiscent of spiny chestnut burrs, cover the buds and hips of the Chestnut rose (Rosa roxburghii; page 106).*

LEFT: *Rosa sericea pteracantha (page 106), growing here with 'Claridge Druce' geranium, has huge wedged thorns that march up the canes with scarcely a space between them. On new canes, the thorns are translucent and glow beautifully when backlit.*

BOTTOM LEFT: *The Cherokee rose (Rosa laevigata) is widely naturalized throughout the southeastern United States; it has been made the state flower of Georgia. Hidden beneath its abundant elegant blossoms and lacquered-looking leaves are plenty of hooked thorns.*

BOTTOM RIGHT: Rosa setigera, *the Prairie rose, is a North American native. Like several of the other native roses— including* R. virginiana, R. carolina, *and* R. arkansana—*it produces bountiful crops of red hips in fall. Its vigor is best directed vertically unless you have a large garden.*

CHAPTER TWO

Growing Healthy Roses

GROWING HEALTHY ROSES isn't really as complicated as people used to think. Forget about becoming an expert on spraying pesticides and fungicides; the excitement about chemicals is waning. In truth, like every other plant, roses need sunshine and water. They are fussy to the extent that they like quite a lot of both, and they like good drainage—usually easily supplied by digging in lots of compost—and, if you want big bushes and an abundance of showy flowers, some nitrogen-rich fertilizer. ❧ The time people used to spend pumping and cleaning sprayers you can spend lazily walking by your roses, looking out for any pests and diseases and picking off the occasional bugs or chewed leaves. Now you are pretty much advised about the hard work required. ❧ This chapter covers all that plus how to shop for roses that grow well in your climate, how to plant, special care in winter, and tips for creating beautiful displays of roses indoors once your garden is bursting with them.

The healthy, handsome foliage of species rose R. glauca.

Shopping for Roses

If you shop wisely for rose plants, you'll be well on your way to a successful rose garden. Strong, healthy, top-grade plants make the fastest start. Varieties well-suited to your climate will help ensure an easy-care garden for years to come.

WHERE TO SHOP

Mail-order catalogs offer the widest choice of roses; they are practically the only way to shop if you are looking for lesser-known roses. You'll also find roses for sale in local nurseries and garden centers, in home-improvement and hardware stores, and even in some supermarkets.

Although you can't examine plants you buy from a catalog until the package arrives, don't let that deter you. Good mail-order suppliers' reputations are based on providing quality plants and service. And don't be put off by the idea of receiving a dormant rose plant with no soil on its roots (the way mail-order houses typically send them to you). It doesn't harm the rose to be dug up and shipped like that, and bare-root plants have advantages over plants sold in containers; see the chart on the next page. For names and addresses of a number of mail-order suppliers, turn to page 126.

A good local nursery or garden center usually stocks roses that do especially well in your area. Large retail chains are more likely to carry the current national best-sellers. During winter and early spring, the roses in these outlets are usually sold as bare-root plants; later in the season, they sell the plants potted in containers.

You can start your rose garden with bare-root plants or plants grown in containers. Bare-root is usually the choice of experienced rose growers, but it's really a matter of what works better for you. The chart on the next page compares the two options.

Where the Plants You Buy Are Grown

Most rose plants are grown in fields in California's San Joaquin Valley—millions of them in rows that stretch as far as the eye can see. During fall, at the end of their second year, they are lifted out of the ground and the soil is shaken from the roots. They are quickly graded and placed in moist cold storage to prevent the roots from drying out. Then they are shipped "bare-root" all over the country—directly to gardeners, to retail outlets, or, in some cases, to wholesale growers who will pot them and grow them on for another year.

Most container-grown roses are potted by the retail outlet, either as soon as the bare-root plants arrive from the grower or else at the end of the bare-root season, when the plants must be either potted or planted in the ground.

WHEN TO SHOP

Container-grown roses are sold almost all year, but, for the widest possible choice of varieties, shop in winter or early spring, as soon as bare-root plants become available in your area. Their arrival should roughly coincide with your earliest planting time (see page 32).

A HEALTHY BARE-ROOT ROSE

A healthy bare-root rose has many thick, green canes (stems); a big cluster of sturdy, fibrous roots; and, if it is budded, a stout, undamaged "bud union" (the swollen, knobby-looking place where the rose was grafted onto the rootstock). Reject any bare-root rose with dried-out or squishy roots or with canes that are weak, shriveled, or beginning to leaf out.

If the plant is packaged in a tube, it may be impossible to inspect the roots before you unpack it. Return the plant to the seller if the roots turn out to be dry—dry roots, more than anything else, lead to trouble.

A HEALTHY CONTAINER-GROWN ROSE

A healthy container-grown rose has flower buds, strong new growth, healthy foliage, and a firm rootball of moist, fibrous roots (ask someone who works at the retail outlet to show the rootball to you). It should be in a large (3- or 5-gallon) container—if it's in a smaller one, the roots were probably cut back hard to fit the pot.

Avoid any plant with roots protruding from the bottom of the container or coiling around the rootball. Also avoid any plant with dieback or weak, straggly growth. These are all signs that the rose has been in the container too long, and this means that it may not establish well in your garden.

WHETHER TO BUY BARE-ROOT OR CONTAINER-GROWN ROSES

BARE-ROOT ROSES	CONTAINER-GROWN ROSES
Available only during winter and early spring	Available almost year-round
Generally less expensive than roses sold in containers	Foliage, flowers, fragrance, vigor on display
Easier to carry home	Easier to store before planting
Need to be planted before they break dormancy, in early spring	Can be planted at almost any time
May establish vigorous roots faster	Provide an instant rose garden

A healthy bare-root rose.

An inferior bare-root rose.

A healthy container-grown rose.

An inferior container-grown rose.

Budded and Own-Root Roses

Most modern roses are not grown on their own roots. To produce reliably vigorous plants, commercial growers raise a special variety, often 'Dr. Huey', for the rootstock, and then graft a bud of 'Peace' (or 'Queen Elizabeth', or any one of the hundreds of rose varieties they sell) into the cane bark of the rootstock plant. If the graft is successful, the bud swells, opens, and gives rise to a whole framework of 'Peace' canes, foliage, and flowers. The top of the rootstock plant is then cut back to the bud union, the place where the 'Peace' bud was inserted.

Many historic and shrub roses, in contrast, are grown on their own roots—as are miniatures.

WHICH GRADE TO BUY

Commercial growers must grade their budded roses according to the number and thickness of the canes. There are three grades: 1, 1½, and 2. Grade 1 roses are the best. They have the greatest number of thick, vigorous canes and are likely to grow into the best bushes. Grade 1½ roses have fewer and thinner canes. Grade 2 plants aren't worth buying even if they are heavily discounted, most gardeners believe.

Roses growing on their own roots are typically smaller to start with than budded roses. They may be graded 3X, 2X, and 1X; the best grade is 3X.

AARS AWARDS

Roses that win an AARS (All-America Rose Selections) award are vigorous plants that perform well in a wide range of climates. These roses have been grown for 2 years in test gardens throughout the United States by the AARS, a nonprofit research organization; of all the new varieties entered in the trials, they have received the most votes in secret-ballot elections.

However, the absence of an AARS award—only three or four are given each year—does not automatically brand a rose as inferior. First, not all new varieties are entered in the trials, so excellent roses can reach the market without AARS testing. And second, some roses, whether or not they have been entered in AARS trials, perform superbly in certain climates or regions but are outclassed by other roses elsewhere.

STORING ROSES

Plant bare-root roses as soon as possible, or the roots may dry out or start growing in the package. If you can't plant right away, because the ground is frozen or too wet, keep the packing around the roots moist, and set the plants in a cool area out of sunlight, such as a garage. In a warm, light place, the roots and shoots may start to grow.

You can store bare-root plants in this way for up to 2 weeks. If you still can't plant, remove the packaging, and place the roses in a dishpan or bucket of moist soil or compost, so that the roots and bud union (for budded roses) are covered. Pack the soil around the plants, and return them to a cool, dim place; keep the soil moist.

To store container-grown roses, place them in a sunny place sheltered from wind. Water them regularly (the soil should always be damp) until you can plant them.

Storing a bare-root rose.

CLIMATE MATTERS

Try not to fall in love with any rose until you know how it does in your climate. Love can turn quickly to disillusionment and sorrow if you have to constantly nurse the poor rose just to keep it alive. Check the advice below and on the following pages to learn which roses suit your climate and which ones spell trouble. To be as sure as you can about whether a particular rose will thrive in your garden, contact someone at a local nursery or rose society who has grown that variety.

COLD-TOLERANT ROSES

Although any rose has a fighting chance of surviving anywhere if you give it enough winter protection (see "The Minnesota Tip," on page 51), you can make your life easier and reduce your disappointments by growing varieties that are hardy in your climate.

If you live where winter temperatures drop below −30°F/ −34°C, choose the most cold-tolerant varieties. The hardiest rose in this book is *Rosa rugosa,* page 106. The popular hybrid rugosa roses listed in "Landscape Roses," on pages 86–100, are just as hardy, or almost. Also consider the Iowa-bred Dr. Griffith Buck hybrids and the Explorer roses, bred to survive southern Canadian winters unprotected. In the descriptions of the recommended roses on pages 74–120, look for the words "good winter hardiness."

Choosing Flower Color

Often, a rose looks striking because the color of its flowers so beautifully suits the surroundings. When you're choosing a rose to plant near your house, make sure its flowers complement the colors of the walls and trim. In fact, consider the background wherever you plant a rose—whether next to a gate, against a fence, or in a multicolored shrub planting.

Any rose looks excellent with a quiet, neutral, or plain background such as a weathered wood fence, a stone wall, or a boxwood hedge. Soft pink roses are usually particularly pleasing with old brick (new brick often has a harsh color that's difficult to work with). Warm-colored pink, orange, red, and yellow roses can take the chill off a cold-looking gray or white wall.

A good match: soft apricot against painted brick.

On a hot patio, white and other pale-colored roses make the brightness seem cooler during the day, and they glow as night falls. Light-colored roses are also easier to use than strong-hued ones in flower borders, since they are more likely to blend with what's there already. (For examples of superb mixed plantings, see pages 10–13.)

In regions where winter temperatures stay above −20°F/ −29°C, you can probably also grow the alba and gallica old garden roses without protection and any of the hybrid kordesii climbing roses. Bear in mind that hardiness is not a precise science— the pattern of cold snaps and thaws affects hardiness, for example.

Hybrid teas and grandifloras generally do not tolerate temperatures below 20°F/−6°C without protection. Shrubs are typically hardier. Listed in the chart on page 29 are modern roses that show unusual hardiness (but they still need protection in cold-winter climates). The list was composed from several sources.

Rose canes tied securely to supports for the winter in New York.

CLOCKWISE FROM TOP LEFT: *'Blaze' is thriving in the dry heat of Santa Fe, New Mexico; good disease resistance makes 'Just Joey' a beautiful candidate for gardens in humid climates; vivid roses brighten a garden on a foggy afternoon; 'The Fairy' offers a profusion of small blossoms in a lightly shaded garden area.*

HEAT-TOLERANT ROSES

Heat can stress roses. The plants may stop growing, the production of flowers may slow down, the blossom colors may bleach or deepen, the flowers of varieties with few petals may "blow" (open too quickly), and the foliage may burn.

Where summers are hot, plant heat-sensitive roses in a spot that's lightly shaded in the afternoon. Keep your roses deeply watered so they continue to grow and bloom through the summer. Consider densely petaled roses such as the centifolias, which perform well only in warm climates. Or see the chart for a list of heat lovers, gathered from recommendations by Kathleen Brenzel in California and Russ Bowermaster in Florida.

HUMIDITY-TOLERANT ROSES

Humidity makes roses more susceptible to diseases, particularly black spot, powdery mildew, and rust (see pages 46–49). If you garden in a humid climate, be sure to select varieties that are not especially prone to these diseases, and plant them in sites with good air circulation (bear in mind that almost no rose is so disease resistant that it is never subject to disease). The list in the chart is composed of recommendations by Russ Bowermaster in Florida and Michael Ruggiero in New York City.

ROSES FOR COOL SUMMERS

Cool, moist air doesn't suit densely petaled roses such as the centifolias; the flowers ball up and fail to open. Either avoid those kinds or try one in the warmest spot of your garden, say against a south- or west-facing wall. Look for roses noted for their disease resistance, because fungal diseases such as black spot, powdery mildew, and rust (see pages 46–49) are common in cool-summer regions. Peggy Van Allen, in the Northwest, recommends all the rugosa roses and also her other favorites listed in the chart.

ROSES FOR SHADY PLACES

Most roses require 6 hours of sunshine a day to thrive. But you can enjoy roses in areas that are marginally shady (not fully shaded). Alba roses (see pages 101–107) do well in lightly shaded spots, as do the varieties listed in the chart.

Cold-Tolerant Roses*	Heat-Tolerant Roses	Humidity-Tolerant Roses	Roses for Cool Summers	Roses for Shady Places
PINK ROSES				
Betty Prior, p. 87	*Cécile Brünner, p. 109*	*Blossomtime, p. 109*	*Ballerina, p. 87*	*Betty Prior, p. 87*
New Dawn, p. 112	*Flower Carpet, p. 90*	*Classic Touch, p. 75*		*Kathleen, p. 92*
Pink Peace, p. 82	*Souvenir de la*	*Playgirl, p. 96*		*New Dawn, p. 112*
Sexy Rexy, p. 98	* Malmaison, p. 107*	*Rosarium Uetersen,*		*The Fairy, p. 100*
The Fairy, p. 100		* p. 113*		
		Sarah Van Fleet, p. 98		
		The Fairy, p. 100		
RED ROSES				
Altissimo, p. 108	*Blaze, p. 108*	*Hunter, p. 93*	*Dortmund, p. 110*	*Altissimo, p. 108*
Knock Out, p. 93	*Europeana, p. 90*	*Knock Out, p. 93*	*Ingrid Bergman, p. 78*	*Knock Out, p. 93*
Loving Memory, p. 79	*Miss Flippins, p. 118*	*Olympiad, p. 81*	*Love, p. 79*	
Mister Lincoln, p. 80	*Mister Lincoln, p. 80*	*Robusta, p. 97*	*Olympiad, p. 81*	
Oklahoma, p. 81	*Olympiad, p. 81*	*Roseraie de l'Hay,*	*Opening Night, p. 81*	
Uncle Joe, p. 85	*Proud Land, p. 82*	* p. 97*		
	Uncle Joe, p. 85			
YELLOW ROSES				
Arthur Bell, p. 89	*Fairhope, p. 115*	*Golden Wings, p. 91*	*Mrs. Oakley Fisher,*	*Alberic Barbier,*
Golden Wings, p. 91	*Midas Touch, p. 80*	*Maigold, p. 111*	* p. 80*	* pp. 65, 69*
Gold Medal, p. 77	*Morning Has Broken,*	*Molineux, p. 95*	*Sunsprite, p. 99*	
Sunsprite, p. 99	* p. 95*			
	St. Patrick, p. 83			
WHITE ROSES				
Iceberg, p. 92	*Green rose, p. 103*	*Gourmet Popcorn,*	*Iceberg, p. 92*	*Kiftsgate, p. 111*
Snow Bride, p. 119	*Iceberg, p. 92*	* p. 116*	*Sally Holmes, p. 97*	*Prosperity, p. 97*
	Nicole, p. 95	*Moonstone, p. 80*		*Sally Holmes, p. 97*
	Sombreuil, p. 113	*Sea Foam, p. 98*		
	White Flower Carpet,	*White Dawn, p. 113*		
	* p. 90*			
OTHERS				
Peace, p. 82	*Fourth of July, p. 110*	*Buff Beauty, p. 88*	*Intrigue, p. 93*	*Eugène de Beauharnais,*
Playboy, p. 96	*Louise Estes, p. 79*	*Cardinal de Richelieu,*	*Stephens' Big Purple,*	* p. 103*
Tropicana, p. 85	*Rosa rugosa, p. 106*	* p. 101*	* p. 83*	*Kordes' Perfecta, p. 78*
		Fourth of July, p. 110	*Sunset Celebration,*	
		Jean Kenneally, p. 117	* p. 84*	
		Just Joey, p. 78		
		Rosa rugosa, p. 106		
		Tamora, p. 100		

*Hardier roses are discussed on page 27.

Getting the Site Ready

Growing roses starts with good siting and good soil. Although roses aren't as fussy as people say, they do perform much better if you plant them in a sunny area and make an excellent home for their roots.

WHAT ROSES NEED

Roses need sunshine, little or no wind, and a fast-draining but moisture-retentive soil that's neither too acidic nor too alkaline.

SUNSHINE AND LITTLE WIND

Choose a planting place where your rose will receive at least 6 hours of sunshine daily. If your weather is consistently cool or overcast, choose a place that's open all day to any sun that might appear. If summer heat is intense, find a spot that receives filtered sunlight during the hottest afternoon hours. Some roses are able to thrive in partial shade (see page 29).

Avoid windy locations. Wind spoils the flowers and increases transpiration from the leaves, so that you need to water more often.

MOISTURE-RETENTIVE, FAST-DRAINING SOIL To make your soil more moisture retentive, add organic matter. It acts as a sponge, slowing the passage of water and dissolved nutrients so that they are available to the rose roots longer.

To find out how fast your soil drains, do a simple test: Dig a hole about 1½ feet deep in the planting area, and fill it with water. If water remains in the hole after 8 hours, the soil drains poorly.

To remedy poor drainage, you have two options: plant your roses in raised beds, which is the plan surest to succeed; or dig the planting area deeply, and add lots of organic matter, which creates air spaces so that the water can penetrate more easily through the soil.

A MODERATE SOIL pH Soils with a pH number less than 7 are acid; those with a pH of 7 are neutral; and those with a pH above 7 are alkaline. Roses grow well in soils that are moderately acid, from about 6.3 to 6.8.

The soil test kits sold at nurseries and garden centers will give you a reading accurate enough to tell whether your soil is extremely acidic or alkaline. You can amend highly acidic soils with lime, strongly alkaline ones with sulfur. Add these amendments as you prepare the soil, following the package instructions. (To be on the safe side, if you suspect you have a major imbalance, you may want to consult a soil lab or local agricultural extension; the experts there will be able to give you specific advice on your problem.)

Raised Beds—the Easy Solution

A stone raised bed adds elegance and height to this rose hedge.

There's a simple solution to dealing with soil that is too shallow or drains poorly: heap soil on top of it and grow your roses above grade. To form the sides of a raised bed, use landscape timbers, decay-resistant wood, brick, concrete block, or stone; or simply make a firm mound with sloping sides and a surrounding ditch. Plan to have the soil surface within the raised bed 1 foot or more above the normal grade outside.

Dig a 4-inch layer of organic material into the existing soil, going down a foot or more if you can. Then add topsoil (taken from another part of the garden or purchased), and dig it into the improved native soil, adding another 4-inch layer of organic matter at the same time. Water the bed deeply and let it settle before you plant it. If it sinks significantly, mix more topsoil into the bed.

HOW TO PREPARE THE SOIL

The big question as you set about preparing for planting is this: Must you dig up and add organic matter to the entire planting area, or can you just dig it into the soil in the planting hole. The answer depends on your soil type.

AMENDING A PLANTING AREA

If your soil drains poorly, work organic matter into the entire planting area, not just the planting hole. Otherwise, the soil in the hole will absorb water from the surrounding soil, and the area around the rose's roots will become waterlogged.

AMENDING SOIL IN A PLANTING HOLE

You can amend just the soil in the planting hole if your purpose is only to make the soil more moisture retentive (always a good idea, even if the soil isn't very sandy), but make the hole big, at least 2 feet wide and 1½ feet deep.

Remove the soil from the planting hole, and mix it with organic material—as much organic matter as you have soil if the soil is very sandy. Set the rose in the hole (see the next pages), and fill in around it with the improved soil.

To amend a planting area, begin by digging or tilling the soil, ideally to a depth of 12 to 18 inches.

IS YOUR SOIL GOOD ENOUGH?

If your garden soil is growing good vegetables (or crops of husky weeds), it will probably grow good roses just as it is.

TYPES OF ORGANIC MATTER

All types of organic material—homemade compost, sawdust, steer manure, leaf mold, shredded bark, and so on—are suitable for improving soil. If you are buying wood by-products such as sawdust and bark, which are not decomposed, make sure nitrogen has been added; otherwise, they'll steal nitrogen from the soil as they decompose. Fresh animal manure will burn rose roots; if you use it, prepare the soil a few months ahead of planting, so the manure has time to decompose.

Spread a layer of organic matter several inches deep over the soil surface, and dig or till it in, until it is thoroughly blended with the soil.

Water the area, and then let the amended soil settle for at least a week before you plant.

Planting Your Roses

It's natural for roses to grow. Help them along by planting them at the right time and deep enough to survive the winter. Be sure to take care of the rose's roots—don't let them dry out.

WHEN TO PLANT

The best time to plant roses depends on your climate and whether you are starting with bare-root roses or container-grown plants.

SCHEDULE FOR BARE-ROOT ROSES

Plant bare-root roses at any time during the dormant season provided your soil is not frozen or waterlogged. January and February are the prime planting months in much of the South, Southwest, and West Coast, where winter temperatures seldom dip below 10°F/−12°C. In regions where subfreezing temperatures alternate with warm spells, and freezing weather can last for many months, late fall and early spring are the best planting times. In decidedly cold-winter regions, you need to plant in spring.

SCHEDULE FOR CONTAINER-GROWN ROSES

You can plant container-grown roses during much of the year—as soon as they are available in winter, provided the ground is not frozen, and on through to fall in mild regions. The best time is spring, when the plants have the longest growing season ahead in which to get established.

If you plant during hot weather, be sure to water your roses frequently.

PLANTING AT THE PROPER DEPTH

Planting a rose at the right depth is always important, but it's of special concern in cold-winter climates—especially if you're planting a budded rose.

BUDDED ROSES Some gardeners keep the bud union above ground; others bury it 1 or 2 inches or even more. The reasoning is this: Exposed to air and sunlight, the bud union tends to produce more canes, but in cold-winter climates an exposed bud union (even when well-protected) is more vulnerable to freezes.

In mild-winter regions where temperatures are unlikely to fall below 10°F/−12°C, you can safely plant your roses with the bud union at or slightly above soil level.

In colder-winter areas, however, choose one of the two options on the right.

OWN-ROOT ROSES If your rose is growing on its own roots (it has no bud union), planting depth is less critical. Where winters are mild, set the rose so the juncture of roots and canes is even with or slightly below the soil level. In cold-winter areas, set the juncture about 1 inch below the soil.

More Canes

Position the bud union just above soil level, and then protect the plants heavily during winter or tip and bury them under the soil (the Minnesota tip; see page 51).

More Protected

Position the bud union 1 to 2 inches (some rosarians recommend as much as 4 inches) below soil level. This is a better guarantee of survival than the first option, but cane production may be less robust.

ALLOWING GENEROUS SPACE

Roses perform best, are less prone to disease, and are easier to maintain when they are not crowded.

Space hybrid teas and grandi-floras 2 to 8 feet apart. Use the 2-foot spacing in very-cold-winter regions where the growing season lasts just 3 to 4 months and roses generally don't grow large. Space 3 feet apart in the warmer parts of the West, Southwest, and South; space 4 to 8 feet apart, depending on the variety, where there's little or no frost to enforce winter dormancy and roses grow prodigiously (much of Florida, the Gulf Coast, California, and parts of Arizona).

Space floribundas (which are usually smaller than hybrid teas and grandifloras) 1½ to 3 feet apart; plant small-growing minia-tures from 1 to 1½ feet apart, and the larger-growing ones 2 to 3 feet apart. Use the closer spacing in colder regions, the widest one where winters are mild.

Rose species (wild roses), shrub roses, and old garden roses need the most room. Allow 5 to 6 feet between plants where winters are cold and long, and up to twice that distance in the mildest areas. In any climate, allow a bit more room for varieties with long, arching canes.

GOOD PLANTING WEATHER

A perfect planting day is calm and overcast, because strong breezes and bright sunlight dry out rose canes and roots.

PLANTING A BARE-ROOT ROSE

It's easy to plant a bare-root rose successfully. First, prepare the soil (see pages 30–31). Until you are ready to put the rose in the ground, keep the roots in water or cover them with a damp cloth so they don't dry out. To plant, follow these steps:

1 Soak the roots in a bucket of water for up to 24 hours before planting, to replenish any moisture they may have lost during transportation and storage. If the rose looks thoroughly dry and shriveled, you might try to plump it back to health by immersing the *entire plant* in water for 24 hours.

2 Dig a large planting hole with sides that slope outward from top to bottom (save the removed soil for step 3). The hole's sides should be rough, not smoothly sculpted. Leave a "plateau" of undug soil at the center of the hole to keep the rose from set-tling too low. Dig the edges deeper to help the roots penetrate into the soil.

3 Form a firm cone of soil over the plateau at the bottom of the hole. Trim any damaged roots or canes from the rose; then place it in the hole, spreading the roots over the soil cone. Put a stick across the hole to gauge the proper planting depth (see "Planting at the Proper Depth," on the opposite page). Fill in the hole with soil, and water well. If the plant settles, raise it gently, and fill in with more soil. Some gardeners mound mulch over the rose for a few weeks to prevent moisture loss from the canes.

PLANTING A CONTAINER-GROWN ROSE

Container-grown roses are even easier to plant than bare-root ones. First, prepare the soil (see pages 30–31). Before planting, water the rose (still in its pot) thoroughly. To keep the roots moist, don't leave the rootball exposed during the planting process for any longer than necessary. To plant, follow these steps:

1 Dig a large planting hole with sides that slope outward from top to bottom (save the removed soil for step 3). The hole's sides should be rough, not smoothly sculpted. Leave a "plateau" of undug soil at the center of the hole to keep the rose from settling too low. Dig the edges deeper to help the roots penetrate into the soil.

2 Take the rose out of its container. If it doesn't slide out easily, lay the container on its side, and gently roll it from side to side to loosen the rose, or tap the pot's sides or bottom sharply, or run a knife around the inside edge. With your fingers, loosen the soil on the surface of the rootball, and uncoil any circling or twisted roots.

3 Set the rose in the planting hole on the soil plateau. Spread out the loosened roots. Add soil beneath the rootball, if needed, to adjust the planting depth (see "Planting at the Proper Depth," on page 32). Fill in the hole with soil, and water well. If the plant settles, raise it gently, and fill in with more soil.

PLANTING MINIATURE ROSES

Most miniatures are small-scale descendants of larger bush roses; they're virtually always grown on their own roots and sold in containers. Plant them as you would a regular container-grown rose, but set them slightly lower than they were in their nursery containers to encourage more roots to form. Because they have shallow root systems, you need to keep the soil constantly moist after planting.

The miniatures known as pot minis, tiny roses sold already flowering in 2½- or 4-inch pots, have spent their lives in green-houses. Before you plant them outdoors, get them used to out-door temperatures gradually, moving them out to a sheltered spot for a few hours every day for several days. Plant them in a container (at least 6 inches deep) or in the ground, as instructed above for regular minis. Water them more frequently though.

PLANTING AND STAKING STANDARD ROSES

Standard roses must be staked at planting time. Choose a sturdy stake that is 2 feet longer than the stem of the standard, measuring from just beneath the bud union at the top of the stem to the soil level in the nursery can—or, if your rose is bare-root, to the old soil level on the stem.

Follow the general planting instructions on pages 32–33, but install the stake before you place the plant in the hole. Drive it 2

Staking a standard.

feet into the ground, just off the center of the hole, on the side of the prevailing wind—place your back to the prevailing wind as you face the hole, and set the stake on your side of center. This way, when the wind blows, the stem will lean away from the stake and not thrash against it.

After planting, check that the top of the stake sits just below the bud union. Because the bud union is vulnerable to damage, it should be clear of the stake.

Tie the stem to the stake in two places: once near the top of the stem, and again halfway up it. Use a figure 8 tie or any other kind of tie that will keep the stem from rubbing against the stake.

Planting a Climber

Check whether your plant is a rambler. If it is, you may prune it back low to the ground before planting it, thus encouraging it to produce strong new shoots from the base. If it's any other type of climber, however, don't prune it before planting.

Follow the general planting instructions on pages 32–33, but make these adjustments: Make your planting hole about 1½ feet away from the wall, arbor, or post. Set the plant at a 45° angle, so the canes lean toward the support. If you are planting against a wall, spread all the roots, as best you can, away from the wall.

Use temporary stakes, as shown at left, to support canes that are too short to reach a trellis or the wire supports on a wall. Push the stakes into the soil at the base of the plant and secure them to the trellis or wire. Then tie the canes to the stakes.

Growing Roses in Containers

Roses thrive in containers. You just need to spend a little time choosing suitable roses and the right containers for them.

CHOOSING A ROSE

Roses with small or moderate growth habits grow more happily in containers than large roses do. Choose miniatures, polyanthas, floribundas, patio roses, or small shrub roses. You'll find a list of varieties recommended for containers on page 9.

CHOOSING A POT THAT'S BIG ENOUGH

Miniature roses thrive in containers as small as a 2-gallon nursery can. But regular-size bushes, standard roses, and climbers need large containers to give their roots room to develop well. A container roughly the size of a 5-gallon nursery can is the very smallest you should consider, and bigger ones are much better. Wooden half-barrels offer plenty of space—even enough room to plant annuals beneath the rose.

ALLOWING FOR GOOD DRAINAGE

Any container you choose must have drainage holes. Use an electric or hand drill to make holes in wood or plastic containers; for clay and concrete, use an electric drill with a masonry or carbide bit. One or two $\frac{1}{2}$-inch holes are sufficient for a small container; for a half-barrel, drill four or five $\frac{3}{4}$-inch holes. To prevent cracking, drill with a small bit first, then increase the bit size until you have made the hole as big as you want.

Be sure there's space beneath your container for water to drain away. If necessary, raise it on small blocks of wood or sit it on pot "feet" that you can buy for this purpose. Keeping the container off the floor also helps prevent water stains on decks and patios. Saucers are even more effective at keeping water off a surface that might stain, but be sure to empty them so that the soil in the pot doesn't get soggy.

Choosing an Attractive Container

Choose a container that will look attractive when the rose you've chosen is planted and the pot is set in place—on the deck, atop a wall, gracing the front steps. If you are not adept at creating beautiful compositions with unusual pots, choose a simple container made of wood or glazed terra-cotta. The natural, earthy colors of these materials show off the beauty of any rose and fit well into most settings.

To be more playful, match the container to elements in its surroundings—steel to echo steel furniture or handrails, blue-glazed clay to match a blue door. Be wary about choosing a multicolored pot or one with a very decorative pattern; when the rose is blooming, the combination of pot and plant may look fussy.

Think twice before you buy a container with a narrow neck—you may have to break it when the rose needs repotting. In hot-summer climates, avoid black containers, which absorb heat and scorch roots. Also steer clear of unglazed terra-cotta pots—they are porous, so you'll need to water more to compensate for moisture lost to evaporation.

BEST PLANTING TIME

The best time to plant a rose in a container is spring. Then the roots have a chance to become established before summer heat arrives.

PLANTING THE ROSE

You can plant either container-grown roses or bare-root roses in a container. For soil, buy a bagged potting mix from a local garden center or nursery. These mixes are guaranteed to retain moisture and also to drain well, which is important for roses.

A CONTAINER-GROWN ROSE

Water the rose thoroughly, and then remove it from its nursery container. If it doesn't slide out easily, lay the container on its side, and gently roll it from side to side to loosen the rose, or tap the pot's sides or bottom sharply, or run a knife around the inside edge. With your fingers, loosen the soil on the surface of the rootball, and uncoil any circling or twisted roots. Then follow the steps on the right.

A BARE-ROOT ROSE

Soak the rose's roots in a bucket of water for up to 24 hours before planting, to replenish any moisture they may have lost. If the rose looks thoroughly dry and shriveled, you might try to plump it back to health by immersing the *entire plant* in water for 24 hours.

If the roots are a little too long to fit the container, bend them slightly to fit. If they are so long you must coil them to fit, cut them back just enough to eliminate the coiling. Then follow the steps on the right.

1 Pour moist (but not soaking wet) potting mix into the container—enough to hold the top of the rootball about 2 inches below the container rim. Place the rose in the container, and fill in around it with more moist potting mix. Press the mix in firmly.

2 Gently water the newly planted rose until water runs out the drainage holes. If the rose settles more than 2 inches below the rim, grasp it just above the roots, and jiggle it upward to the proper height; then fill in with more soil. Water often to keep the soil moist. Fertilize regularly with a liquid or timed-release fertilizer (see page 41).

1 Pour moist (but not soaking wet) potting mix into the container so that it forms a firm cone—high enough to hold the bud union (or, if the rose is not budded, the juncture of roots and canes) about 2 inches below the container rim.

2 Spread the roots over the cone, and fill in around them with more moist potting mix. Fill the container to within 2 inches of the rim. Press the mix in firmly. Then follow step 2 for "A Container-Grown Rose," above.

Watering Your Roses

To perform well, roses need moisture all the way down through their root zone, all through the year. Water them deeply and consistently.

HOW MUCH TO WATER

A rose needs water to the full depth of its roots (assume 16 to 18 inches), in enough quantity to keep the soil constantly moist but not waterlogged. Grown without enough water, the plant will be smaller, the flowers will be smaller, and the blooming season will be shorter.

We can't tell you how many gallons to apply, because the amount varies enormously, according to whether the soil is sandy (needs more water) or mostly clay. To figure out how much water it takes to wet your soil, a day after you water dig a hole to see how far the moisture has penetrated.

The first sign of underwatering is wilting shoots at the top of the bush. Overwatering, without sufficient drainage, causes the lower leaves to turn yellow and drop.

HOW OFTEN TO WATER

Soil type also plays a role in how often roses need watering. During "average" spring weather, roses growing in sandy soil may need watering every 5 days, those in loam every 7 to 10 days, and those in clay every other week. Roses need less frequent watering if it rains or if you mulch (see the box on the left). They need more frequent watering if the weather is windy, hot, or sunny.

If you don't know your soil well, water deeply—in fact, always water deeply; light sprinkling does no good—so that the entire root zone is moist, and check the soil 4 or 5 days later: Dig a small hole with a trowel. If the soil is moist at a depth of 2 to 3 inches, don't water yet; if it's dry, turn on the water now.

Once you've checked your soil on a few occasions, you'll get a sense of how often to water. Remember to water in the dormant season, as necessary, for as long as the soil is not frozen.

Mulching Conserves Water

Placing an organic mulch around your roses keeps the soil cool and moist, so you don't have to water as often; it also suppresses weeds and provides nutrients to the soil as it decomposes. Mulching roses is altogether a very good idea.

Organic mulches include homemade compost, pine needles (although they acidify the soil), shredded leaves from hardwood trees (oak leaves, for instance), redwood bark, sawdust, rice hulls, ground corn cobs, well-rotted manure, and lawn clippings (as long as they are free of herbicide and grass and weed seeds). In windy spots, avoid lightweight mulches like straw. If you use corn cobs or undecomposed wood products such as bark or sawdust, sprinkle a high-nitrogen fertilizer over the soil surface to replace the nitrogen that the mulch will steal from the soil as it decays.

A straw mulch.

Spread the mulch in early spring. In cold-winter regions, wait until the soil has warmed; if you spread mulch too early it will delay soil warming and will slow growth. Make a layer 2 to 3 inches thick, extending it to within an inch of the base of the rose. Add more mulch when necessary to keep the layer thick.

Generally, it's best to water just the soil, not the rose foliage, because many fungal diseases that attack the leaves, like black spot, flourish in a damp environment. If you want to hose the leaves to remove dust, aphids, or mites, do it early on a sunny day so that the leaves won't stay damp for long.

HOW TO WATER

Most gardeners use some form of irrigation. Even when it rains in the summer, rainfall is not always sufficient to penetrate deep into the soil, where the rose roots are.

FLOOD BASINS Flood basins are the low-cost option. Around each bush, build an earthen dike 2 to 6 inches high and about 3 feet across. When it's time to irrigate, gently flood the basins, using a hose. If you dislike the look of the basins, spread a mulch in and between them, or, if the soil is level, forget the individual basins and instead surround the entire rose bed with a berm.

DRIP IRRIGATION Drip irrigation consists of lines of flexible black tubing and emitters that release water in drips or light sprays. It can be automated and is relatively inexpensive and simple to install. It is usually the best choice if you want to conserve water. To water a rose bed, lay the tubing in parallel rows to soak the whole bed. For widely spaced bushes, snake the tubing to and around the individual plants. Place mulch over the tubing to hide it.

PERMANENT SPRINKLERS A permanent sprinkler system supplied by underground pipes is the costliest option. It lets you automate the irrigation and avoid loops of tubing on the soil surface, but you may need professional help to install it. If roses in your area are prone to fungal diseases, choose bubbler or flat-spray sprinklers, so the foliage doesn't get wet.

Watering Roses in Containers

Roses growing in a container need more frequent watering than roses in the ground. Don't wait for them to wilt. Check the soil often, daily in hot or windy weather. If you find dry soil 2 inches below the surface, water the container immediately.

The rootball may shrink away from the sides of the container if it gets very dry. Plug the gaps with potting soil, and water the rootball slowly or pour water into the saucer and let the rootball absorb it that way.

Feeding Your Roses

Roses won't dwindle away and die without fertilizer, but virtually all modern roses and many of the old garden sorts need at least a little to perform well.

WHEN TO APPLY FERTILIZER

After planting your roses, generally wait until after the first flush of bloom before fertilizing them.

In subsequent years, apply fertilizer soon after you finish pruning, to give the roses a boost for putting out new growth when the growing season begins. Do a follow-up application after the first round of spring bloom. For old garden roses that flower only once, this is the only fertilizer you need apply. For repeat-flowering roses, continue to apply fertilizer through the summer.

HOW OFTEN TO FERTILIZE

How often to fertilize repeat-flowering roses depends mostly on the product you choose. Timed-release fertilizers last many months. Granular fertilizers last longer than liquid ones.

Soil type also affects the situation. Clay holds dissolved nutrients longest, so you can fertilize less frequently. If your soil is sandy, you may want to fertilize more often to compensate for faster leaching of the nutrients.

Heavy rainfall can flush fertilizer from the soil and leave roses short of necessary nutrients.

AN ORGANIC FERTILIZER PROGRAM

Organic fertilizers are derived from the remains of living organisms; examples include bone meal, alfalfa meal, cottonseed meal, blood meal, fish emulsion, and steer manure. Many gardeners prefer them because these materials occur naturally and sustain the natural life of the soil. They have a low percentage of nitrogen (with the exception of blood meal) and release their nutrients slowly, so they are unlikely to cause fertilizer burn or to leach large amounts of nitrates into the groundwater.

Start in spring by spreading an organic mulch rich in nutrients, such as compost or aged manure. Then incorporate alfalfa meal or cottonseed meal or a mix of the two into the soil (see "Dry Fertilizer," on the next page) after the first flowering and again in midsummer. Alternatively, after the mulch, use fish emulsion or seaweed extract regularly through the season; because these are in liquid form, they provide nutrients quickly to the rose's roots.

A SYNTHETIC FERTILIZER PROGRAM

Synthetic fertilizers are manufactured and have names like ammonium sulfate and potassium phosphate. These fertilizers are high in nutrients and can be very fast acting. But they are easily leached from the soil by rainfall or regular heavy irrigation.

The simplest program to follow is regular applications of synthetic "rose food," a complete fertilizer, containing phosphorus and potassium as well as nitrogen. Alternatively, to reduce the number of applications, apply a timed-release synthetic fertilizer in early spring and then just one or two applications of rose food or a plain nitrogen formula in late spring and summer.

EPSOM SALTS

Epsom salts (magnesium sulfate), an old home remedy for aches and pains, has become popular among rose growers, who say it encourages strong new canes to grow from the base of the bush. Apply it along with your other

How to Read a Fertilizer Label

The label on a bag of fertilizer shows the percentages of nutrients in the mix. The three numbers shown most prominently, called the N–P–K ratio, refer to the amounts of nitrogen (N), phosphorus (P), and potassium (K) in the bag. For example, an 8-4-4 fertilizer contains, by weight, 8 percent nitrogen, 4 percent phosphorus, and 4 percent potassium. Nitrogen is the most critical element. It promotes good foliage growth and flowers, and you need to add it to the soil to give roses enough.

fertilizer after pruning, using about ¾ cup for each plant. A second, slightly smaller application after the first flush of bloom may also be beneficial.

WHEN TO STOP FERTILIZING

In cold-winter areas, it's conventional to stop fertilizing for the year sometime during the summer, so that the roses have time to harden off and become properly resistant to cold before winter. The rule of thumb about when to stop is no later than 6 weeks before the expected first frost; that means stopping anywhere between August 1 and early September. (For the expected first-frost date in your area, ask your local nursery.)

In mild-winter areas, gardeners may stop fertilizing in October to encourage winter dormancy. They can then remove the leaves and spray the canes to help keep plants healthy (see page 46). Some gardeners fertilize year-round.

APPLYING FERTILIZER

Before applying fertilizer to the soil, be sure to water first. If you apply fertilizer to dry soil and then water it in, it can burn the rose's surface feeder roots. There are three basic types of fertilizer: dry, liquid, and foliar.

DRY FERTILIZER To apply dry fertilizer, first lightly scratch the soil surface (no more than 1½ inches deep) beneath your rose.

If you mulch, you'll have to move some of the mulch aside. Work as far out as the branches spread, but leave several inches around the base of the rose uncultivated. On the cultivated soil, scatter the amount of fertilizer recommended on the package label; then water again well.

LIQUID FERTILIZER To apply liquid fertilizer to individual roses, mix the fertilizer in a wa-tering can, and apply the recommended amount to each bush.

For larger plantings, consider buying an injector device that lets

you run the fertilizer solution through your watering system. The simplest is a siphon attachment that draws liquid concentrate from a pail into your hose or watering line. Another sort is a small canister that attaches between the faucet and the hose (or drip irrigation line).

FOLIAR FERTILIZER To apply foliar fertilizer, spray the nutrient solution onto the undersides of the rose leaves, where it is quickly absorbed. Use any liquid fertilizer recommended for foliar application. Because foliar fertilizer can burn leaves in hot weather, don't use it when temperatures will reach 80°F/27°C or above.

FERTILIZING CONTAINERS

Roses growing in containers need more fertilizer than roses growing in the ground. Choose a liquid fertilizer or a dry fertilizer, and look for a complete fertilizer with nitrogen, phosphorus, and potassium, plus micronutrients. Apply the fertilizer every 2 weeks, reducing the strength of the solution if necessary to match the recommendations on the package.

Fixing Cultural Problems

Roses grow luxuriantly in most soils, especially if you supply some nitrogen. Occasionally, they suffer from nutrient deficiencies or extreme weather conditions or a lack of proper care or even too much of a good thing. Use the information here to identify and correct the most common cultural problems.

NOT ENOUGH WATER

Stems and leaves droop, starting at the top of the bush. Soak the soil to a depth of 18 inches, and water again, deeply, whenever the soil is dry 2 to 3 inches beneath the surface.

BALLING

Buds fail to open fully; petals turn brown; common among roses with thin petals growing in damp climates. Choose rose varieties carefully (see pages 27–29). Plant in full sun, so moisture doesn't linger in the buds. May also be caused by a heavy infestation of aphids or thrips (see pages 48–49).

NOT ENOUGH IRON

Large yellow areas on leaves (veins stay green); new growth is most affected. Apply an iron chelate fertilizer for fastest results. Most likely caused by a high pH soil (see page 30).

FERTILIZER BURN

Leaf edges or whole leaves turn brown and crisp; growth slows. Water heavily to flush some of the fertilizer out of the soil. Remove burned foliage. Follow the directions on the fertilizer package to determine the correct dose. Always water the soil before applying fertilizer.

NOT ENOUGH PHOSPHORUS

Dark green leaves with purple tints on undersides; leaves drop early. Apply a high-phosphorus fertilizer to the root zone; if you are planting new bushes, mix it into the backfill soil. Check the soil pH (see page 30), which may be the cause of the problem.

NOT ENOUGH NITROGEN

Light green or yellow-green leaves, with some red spots; leaves drop prematurely; slow overall growth; symptoms appear first at base of bush. Apply a nitrogen fertilizer regularly (see pages 40–41). A high-nitrogen foliar fertilizer, sprayed onto the undersides of the leaves, will give the fastest results.

HERBICIDE DAMAGE

Leaves twist and die; new growth is stunted and deformed; the plant may die if the dose was heavy. Should you accidentally spray an herbicide on your bush, hose it off immediately. Once the herbicide is absorbed, the damage is done, and all you can do is cut off the affected growth. Use herbicides only on still, cool mornings, and read the label carefully. Wait at least 2 months before mulching with grass clippings or manure that may contain traces of herbicide. Don't use your watering can to mix or apply herbicides.

SUNBURN

Blackened areas on canes; leaf burn, especially on south and west sides of bush. Excessive heat is the cause. Cut off affected growth. Move the rose away from a reflective surface, such as white masonry or a white rock mulch. To reduce the chances of sunburn, don't let the soil dry out or the bush become defoliated because of pest problems.

NOT ENOUGH MAGNESIUM

Yellowing and dead tissue at the center of leaves; old leaves are most affected. Apply a fertilizer that contains a high level of magnesium or Epsom salts (see page 40).

NOT ENOUGH MANGANESE

Bands of yellow between the leaf veins. Apply a fertilizer that contains chelated micronutrients, including manganese. Check the soil pH (see page 30); if it's above 7.0, that may be the cause of the problem.

TOO MUCH WATER

Leaves turn yellow (first the veins and leaf center) and fall off, starting at the base of the bush. Water only when the soil is dry 2 to 3 inches beneath the surface and only to moisten the dry layer. Check drainage.

NOT ENOUGH POTASSIUM

Brown, brittle edges to old leaves; small flowers. Apply a fertilizer high in potassium, such as potassium nitrate. Check the soil pH (see page 30), which may have caused the problem.

Cutting Roses for Indoors

After working in your garden, bring at least one or two roses indoors with you. If you care for them a little, they'll last long enough to brighten someone's spirits—and inspire you to grow more roses so you can bring dozens inside.

LONG-LASTING BOUQUETS

How long your roses last indoors depends on the rose varieties you are growing (see the box below) and how careful you are with the cutting.

CAREFUL CUTS For the longest-living bouquets, cut your roses early in the morning or in late afternoon to early evening. Choose stems with flower buds that are no more than half open. Make cuts just above a leaf, which will encourage a new stem to grow. Check that the portion of stem you are leaving behind has at least two sets of leaves—cutting too long a stem may weaken your plants.

Carry a bucket of water with you into the garden, and put the cut stems into it immediately. Once you've finished cutting, take the bucket out of the sunlight into a cool place, and fill it with warm water until most of the leaves are submerged and the flowers are just above the water surface. To enhance their freshness, leave the roses immersed like this for about an hour.

Before placing your cut roses in a vase, recut the stems under water, making slanting cuts. Underwater cutting helps prevent air from getting into the stems, which causes bent necks. Remove any foliage that will be underwater in the vase, so it doesn't rot and spoil the water.

AFTERCARE Recut the stems under water every other day, removing about ½ inch of stem each time. To extend the life of the flowers and keep the water looking fresh, use floral preservatives.

HOW MANY TO CUT

If your rose is mature and vigorous, cut as many flowers as you like. With a younger, smaller plant, cut just a few flowers with fairly short stems, or you'll diminish the plant's strength.

Roses for Cutting

Any rose is beautiful indoors. But the most popular roses for cutting—because they have long, strong stems and large flowers and they are easy to maintain in a bouquet—are hybrid teas and grandifloras. The best of those have thick petals (which don't wilt quickly) and blooms that open slowly. Here are a number of proven choices, listed by flower color.

PINK
Bewitched
Bride's Dream
Fame!
Queen Elizabeth

RED
Mister Lincoln
Olympiad
Uncle Joe

ORANGE/WARM
BLENDS
Brandy
Fragrant Cloud
Just Joey
Touch of Class

YELLOW/CREAM
Elina
Gold Medal
Saint Patrick

LAVENDER
Lagerfeld
Paradise

WHITE
Crystalline
Honor
Pascali

MULTICOLOR
Double Delight
Peace

Cut at a 45° angle just above a leaf with five leaflets, preferably one pointing toward the outside of the plant.

How to Display Roses Beautifully

You can show off a single exquisite rose alone, fill a vase with dozens of the same variety, make a duo of roses and one other flower, or include your roses in a bouquet of many different flowers. Try them all, if you have enough roses.

RIGHT: A perfect rose can be an effective arrangement all by itself. Displaying it this way encourages people to discover every detail of its beauty and complexity. Place it where it can be appreciated at close range—beside a sink or on a bedside table, for example.

ABOVE: A mixed bouquet that's predominantly one color is the easiest kind to make. These roses, columbine, and Jupiter's beard are lovely together because they combine a range of pinks, from deep to very light. Green foliage pulls the colors together. White flowers add sparkle and freshness.

ABOVE: This all-of-a-kind 'Pat Austin' rose bouquet looks particularly lavish because it contains more than two dozen roses. For a natural look, flowers in various stages of development have been included. A few geranium leaves soften the rim of the vase and hide the ¼-inch grid of floral tape, which is holding the roses in place.

BELOW: Fluffy white hydrangeas form a bed of clouds for these sweet pink roses. The rose stems are cut fairly short and inserted one by one among the hydrangea heads, which hold them in place without the need for a frog or floral foam. The silver bowl makes a bright, elegant container.

Pests and Diseases

Many sprays kill the good bugs as well as the bad ones. It's often best to tolerate a little damage in order to keep your garden naturally healthy.

CLOCKWISE FROM TOP LEFT: *Black spot, caterpillar, mite damage, cane borer damage, aphids.*

STEP ONE: PREVENT

Well-tended, healthy roses are less likely to fall prey to damaging pest infestations or diseases. Here are eight ways to reduce the risk of trouble:

- Choose roses that are suitable for your climate (see pages 27–29) and that have a natural resistance to disease (check the listings on pages 74–120). Be aware that disease resistance is more common among old roses and shrub roses than among hybrid teas.
- Get your roses off to a good start: choose a sunny, well-drained site, amend the soil, plant at the recommended spacing, and water sufficiently (see pages 30–39).
- Fertilize appropriately, not too little but also not too much—bugs love lush new leaves (see pages 40–41).
- Start the year with a garden cleanup: After pruning, clear the ground of prunings, leaves, and old mulch. Then, before the plants leaf out, spray them and the soil to kill any insect eggs and disease spores (especially black spot); use a combination of horticultural oil and lime-sulfur fungicide. After this preventive spraying, no other sprays may be necessary.
- Encourage beneficial insects (see "Step Three") to make their home in your garden, to feed on aphids and other rose pests.
- Prune your roses to improve air circulation around the foliage, which helps prevent disease.
- Avoid overhead watering and spray heads that splash water from the soil onto the leaves, because water droplets can spread disease spores. If you need to hose off pests, do it early in the day, so the leaves dry quickly; wet leaves are an invitation to black spot and other fungal diseases.
- Inspect your roses frequently, to catch problems early.

STEP TWO: PICK, HOSE, CLEAN UP

A very effective way to control pests on your roses is to pick them off and drop them in a bucket of soapy water. If the bugs are tiny, hose them off with a strong jet of water. The number one rose pest—aphids—can be controlled this way. And it's a sensible, effective first line of defense against spider mites, beetles, cane borers, rose scale, leafhoppers, rose slugs, and caterpillars.

To combat many of the rose diseases, think first of simply picking and disposing of the affected leaves or flowers and cleaning up any fallen leaves or flowers, which may harbor eggs or disease spores.

STEP THREE: SUPPORT THEIR ENEMIES

Many rose pests, including aphids, rose slugs, rose scale, spider mites, grasshoppers, and thrips, have natural enemies that prey on them, such as ladybugs (lady beetles), lacewings, beetles, flies, spiders, birds, and wasps.

Support these predators by finding a place in your garden for their favorite plants, such as fennel, Queen Anne's lace, and yarrow. Avoid broad-spectrum pesticides, which kill the predators as well as the pests. If a spray may be harmful to predators, spray

---

LOCK THEM UP

Young children love to play with liquids and containers, so store *all* of your garden pesticides—even some of the "natural" ones are toxic to humans—out of their reach, preferably under lock and key.

Controlling Pests and Diseases the Natural Way

Here are the most common "natural" products:

INSECTICIDAL SOAP SPRAYS Made from potassium salts of fatty acids, these control soft-bodied pests, such as aphids, in their immature nymph stages.

HORTICULTURAL OILS These refined oils from plants or petroleum smother insects, eggs, and disease spores. Depending on type, they can be used during the growing season or as a dormant spray. Oils may burn leaves, so do not use them if the temperature is expected to exceed 80°F/27°C.

SODIUM BICARBONATE (BAKING SODA) Mixed in water, this is a home remedy for powdery mildew and black spot (see pages 48–49). Keep it out of fish ponds. Also consider commercial products containing potassium bicarbonate.

NEEM A botanical insecticide derived from the bark of a tree native to India, neem repels pests and causes them to stop feeding. It also inhibits black spot and powdery mildew. May be less effective in hot weather.

PYRETHRUM Derived from a chrysanthemum species, this and its more concentrated form, pyrethrin, are highly toxic to insects. Note that the more common pyrethroid products are made from a synthetic chemical; they are more toxic and stay in the environment longer than pyrethrum and pyrethrin.

---

late in the day when they are not active.

Some predators, also known as *beneficial insects* or *biological controls,* can be purchased and released into the rose garden. Ladybugs eat aphids; lacewings attack thrips. Bt *(Bacillus thuringiensis)* is a bacterium that kills caterpillars; milky spore, another bacterium, kills the larvae of Japanese beetles.

CLOCKWISE FROM TOP LEFT: *Thrips damage, grasshopper, powdery mildew, downy mildew.*

It is important to release predators at an appropriate time—for example, not before the pests are present, or the predators will have no food; and only during the pest's larval stage if the predator doesn't touch the adults. You may need to make more than one release. Ask your local nursery or mail-order supplier for advice on timing.

STEP FOUR: USE NATURAL POISONS

Many naturally occurring substances are lethal to pests and diseases. It makes sense to use these before resorting to synthetic poisons, because natural remedies have less impact on the environment. But be sure to read the labels, for these controls are not harmless; many kill beneficial insects and can harm fish. Apply them only if you already have an infestation or have good reason to fear one.

STEP FIVE: CONSIDER SYNTHETIC CHEMICALS

Think of synthetic pesticides as the last resort. Many common ones are toxic to humans, animals, and the beneficial predators in your garden; they may also be approved for use only on ornamental crops, not edible crops, so be extremely careful if you have a vegetable garden near your roses.

If you need to spray with a synthetic chemical to save a rose, look for a substance targeted to the specific pest or disease. Combination products and broad-spectrum sprays that kill everything are avoided by gardeners who treasure the diversity of natural life in their gardens.

Synthetic products can be safe and highly effective when they are used properly. Read the label carefully, wear protective gear as advised, and use the product only as directed—it's against the law to do otherwise.

Controlling Pests and Diseases

Respond quickly to pests and diseases but don't overreact. Once you've identified the problem, using these pages, choose the control least likely to harm the environment and beneficial insects. These controls are listed first.

APHIDS (GREENFLIES)

These soft bodied, $\frac{1}{8}$-inch-long insects may also be red, brown, or black. They cluster on new growth and suck out the sap, which causes damage only if they are present in very high numbers. Hose off with water; purchase and release ladybugs (their natural enemy); spray with insecticidal soap, neem oil, or pyrethrum products if the plant is truly infested.

BEETLES

Several kinds. The Japanese beetle, with bronze body and metallic head, is a serious pest in eastern states. Many other beetles do little damage; some eat holes in buds, petals, and leaves. Handpick; treat the soil and lawn with milky spore (this works for Japanese beetles but not all others); spray with neem oil or a suitable insecticide.

DOWNY MILDEW

Purplish red leaf spots with smudged edges; leaves turn yellow and drop; canes can also become infected. Spores spread in water, overwinter in cane lesions and on old leaves. Warm weather, above 80°F/27°C, kills spores, so you may not need to spray with fungicide. Remove prunings and old leaves. Avoid overhead watering, unless done early in day.

BLACK SPOT

Circular black spots on leaves, sometimes with yellowing around spots. Disease thrives in warmth and is spread by water (rainfall, sprinklers). If left unchecked, it can defoliate a plant. Canes can also become infected. Remove affected leaves and debris; spray with a combination of baking soda and summer-weight horticultural oil (2 teaspoons of each per gallon of water), or neem oil, or a suitable fungicide. Avoid overhead watering. Since spores overwinter, do careful winter cleanup, and apply a preventive spray (see page 46).

RUST

Small orange spots on leaf undersides enlarge to form thick, powdery masses of orange spores; yellow blotches appear on leaf surfaces. If severe, rust can defoliate a plant. Remove affected leaves, clean up debris, avoid overhead watering; spray with a suitable fungicide.

Save the Leafcutter Bee

Leafcutter bees cut semicircular holes in rose leaves and use the material to line their nests. Don't take action against these bees; they serve as important pollinators in the garden.

THRIPS

These nearly invisible insects deform and discolor flower petals by rasping and puncturing the tissue. White and pastel flowers are their favorites. Plants in dry soil are more likely to be attacked, so water properly. Remove affected buds; release lacewings; spray with insecticidal soap, neem oil, or a suitable insecticide.

SPIDER MITES

These tiny spider relatives suck juices from the leaf surface, causing dry-looking, russeted leaves; in heavy infestations, undersides of leaves show silvery webbing. Mites increase rapidly in hot, dry weather. Hose off leaf surfaces and undersides with water regularly during an infestation; spray with horticultural oil (summer weight), insecticidal soap, or neem oil.

SCALE INSECTS

Small, round to oval, grayish crusty scales on canes are unsightly and stunt growth. Scrape off with a nail file; spray with insecticidal soap; spray with horticultural oil in winter (see pages 46–47).

MOSAIC VIRUS

Yellow zigzag, vein clearing, or splotching pattern on leaves; reduced plant vigor and flower production. The virus is transmitted through the budding process, at the commercial grower's nursery. No treatment or cure.

ROSE MIDGES

Tiny fly larvae rasp the tender tips of new growth, causing them to shrivel and blacken. Stop the larvae from pupating in the soil by laying sheets of black plastic under the plants. Remove affected shoots. Clear away leaf litter, weeds, and debris. Try insecticidal soap on the foliage, or spray plants and soil with a suitable insecticide.

POWDERY MILDEW

A fungal disease producing gray to white, furry to powdery coating on new leaves, stems, and flower buds. Leaves become crumpled and distorted. Is encouraged by crowding (poor air circulation), shade, and fog. Spray with a combination of baking soda and horticultural oil (2 teaspoons of each per gallon of water), or neem oil, or a suitable fungicide.

CATERPILLARS AND WORMS

Larvae of various flying insects skeletonize or chew holes in leaves (look for leafroller caterpillars inside a rolled leaf). Handpick; spray with Bt.

CANE BORERS

These worms bore into new shoots or pruned canes and consume the stem's pith. New growth tips wilt and collapse. Handpick by cutting off infected stems and crushing them. Prune canes until you find healthy pith.

Winter Protection

In mild regions, all roses are safe from the risk of winter freeze damage. In much of the country, however, preparing the plants for winter is part of routine rose-garden maintenance.

IS PROTECTION NECESSARY?

Generally speaking, modern hybrid teas, grandifloras, miniatures, and climbers run little risk of damage in areas where winter lows seldom dip below 10°F/−12°C. Some floribundas and many miniature, shrub, and old garden roses can remain unprotected where 0°F/−18°C is a standard low temperature, and a few species and species hybrids are even tougher. Be sure to check the listings on pages 74–120 for information on specific varieties.

Occasional temperatures colder than those minimums may or may not hurt exposed canes. Dry or very cold winds greatly increase the risk of damage. Plants are also more susceptible to winter injury if temperatures fluctuate and the soil freezes, thaws, and refreezes.

SURVIVAL TIPS

The best insurance against winter losses is to buy roses that are hardy in your region (see pages 27 and 29). It makes sense to mound your roses, as additional insurance, if you live in a very-cold-winter climate; you must do it if you are experimenting with marginally hardy roses. You can also minimize the effect of winter cold on your roses in these ways:

- Plant them against a sheltered wall or on the lee side of windbreak shrubs; avoid the most exposed and the lowest-lying spots in the garden, which are the coldest.
- Plant budded roses so that the bud union is protected below ground (see page 32).
- Provide good care to your roses during the growing season;

roses defoliated by pests or diseases are not so well equipped to survive a hard winter.

- Stop deadheading and stop fertilizing 6 weeks before first frosts are expected in your area, so no new growth is produced. Your plants then have a chance to produce hips and go into a protective deep dormancy.
- Be sure to continue watering until the ground freezes. If the roots are well watered, the plants can better resist the desiccating effects of wind.

MOUNDING AND TIPPING

Don't rush to cover or tip your roses too soon. Begin with a thorough cleanup in early or midautumn, clearing away all old leaves and spent flowers, and removing all debris and mulch from around the base of each plant. Then strip away and discard any leaves remaining on the canes, and cut back any dead or diseased canes.

MOUNDING

Cut the canes back to 3 feet, and tie them together; then mound soil at least 1 foot high over the base of the bush. After the soil mound freezes, cover it with an insulating mound of straw, hay, cut conifer boughs, or other noncompacting organic material. To hold the mound in place, surround the bush with a wire mesh cylinder. If you use a rose cone instead of wire mesh, be sure it has ventilation, and weight it down with a brick.

OWN-ROOTS MAY COME BACK

Own-root roses are favorites in very cold climates, because, if the canes die during winter, the roots often send up new replacement canes in spring. Budded roses do the same, but the canes from the roots are of the rootstock variety not the glorious budded variety growing before.

If you are tipping your roses (the most thorough form of protection and usually used only for nonhardy roses in really cold-winter areas), do it before the soil freezes, around midautumn. If you are mounding your plants, you can mound the bases of the plants in early to midautumn, but wait until the soil freezes to apply mulch over the mounds. Just before you expect the soil to freeze, give the roses a deep soaking.

REMOVING PROTECTION

Resist the urge to remove protection at the first sign of spring; temperatures may drop suddenly many times before spring truly arrives. In general, the best time to uncover the plants is the time best for dormant-season pruning in your area (see page 58).

PROTECTING POTTED ROSES

The soil in containers gets much colder in winter than ground soil. If you live in a region where temperatures fall more than a few degrees below freezing, move your pots into an unheated garage or shed (the temperature mustn't fall below 10°F/−12°C). Let the plants go into dormancy, remove any remaining leaves, and water only occasionally. In spring, when all danger of frost is past, take them back outdoors, prune lightly, and start fertilizing them again.

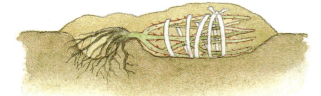

THE MINNESOTA TIP
Make a trench to one side of the rose. Loosen the roots on the side of the plant away from the trench, and bend the plant over into the trench, being careful to bend the roots— not the trunk or it may snap. Cover the roots and the plant with soil.

To tip a standard, loosen the roots on the side opposite the bud union at the base of the trunk. Then bend the plant over the bud union into the trench, being careful to bend the roots—not the trunk or it may snap. Pin the trunk in place, and cover both trunk and canes with soil.

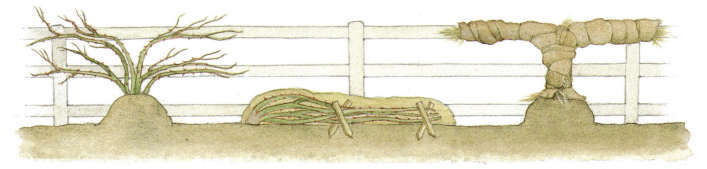

NONHARDY CLIMBERS
Where winter lows range from 5° to 15°F/−15° to −9°C, protect nonhardy climbing roses with soil mounds (left). Where lows will drop below −10°F/−23°C, remove the climbing canes from the supports, pin them, and cover them with soil (center). Where low temperatures fall in the 5° to −10°F/−15° to −23°C range, you can leave the climbing canes in place if you insulate them with straw and then cover the insulated canes with burlap (right).

Propagating Your Roses

With so many roses available for sale, why bother starting your own? Simply the pleasure it brings, is the usual answer: imagine being able to point out a beautiful rose that you nurtured from seed or a piece of stem one spring.

TAKING CUTTINGS

A simple way to propagate roses is to take cuttings during the blooming season. (Using suckers and layering, described on the next page, are even simpler methods but not possible with all roses.) If you haven't already set your heart on propagating a particular variety, take your cuttings from the most vigorous rose you can find, because those have the best chance for success. But remember that it's against the law to propagate a patented rose by cuttings. Most new roses are patented; look for the symbol on the label.

Once you've selected a rose, follow these steps:

1 Choose a strong young shoot that has just flowered. Take an 8-inch-long portion of the stem, cutting just above a leaf at the flower end of the stem and just beneath a leaf at the bottom end. Use very sharp pruners, and make slanting cuts, as shown.

2 Remove the lowest leaves. Dip the bottom end of the stem in rooting hormone. Fill a pot with perlite, and place the stem into it. Water the pot well.

3 Insert a stake into the pot, put the pot into a plastic bag, and tie the top of the bag (the stake keeps the bag upright). Place the pot in a shaded but well-lit spot outdoors. Water only if the cutting wilts; it probably won't need watering until step 4.

4 When new growth shows that the cutting has rooted (within 1 to 2 months), remove the bag gradually, over 7 to 10 days, opening the top just a little to start, and water just enough to keep the leaves from wilting. Place the new plant in the garden during the next planting season.

SOWING SEEDS

Roses grown from seed are rarely as lovely as the parent plant, but it's fun to harvest the rose hips and see what comes up in the seedling tray. You can expect seedlings of bush hybrid teas, grandifloras, floribundas, and miniatures to flower as soon as 6 weeks after germination. Climbing roses and some shrub and old garden roses may not bloom for 2 to 3 years.

Follow these steps:

1 Pick rose hips when they turn from green to red, orange, yellow, or brown; don't wait until they shrivel. Place them in a plastic bag; cover them with damp peat moss or sand; and place them in the vegetable crisper of your refrigerator.

2 After 6 to 8 weeks, the hips will be black and partially decomposed. Take them out of the bag and remove the seeds. To test the seeds for viability, put them in water; sow the ones that sink.

3 Fill individual pots (at least 3 inches deep) with moist seed-starting mix. Sow the seeds ⅜ to ½ inch deep and 2 inches apart. Lightly firm the surface. Germination may start within 6 weeks and continue for 2 months or over a year.

4 In mild-winter regions, you can place the pots outdoors, away from wind and direct sunlight. In cold-winter regions, place the pots in a greenhouse, or indoors on a sunny windowsill or under artificial lights. As soon as the danger of frost is past, take them into a sheltered place outdoors. After a year, you can plant the new roses in the garden, at planting time.

USING SUCKERS AND LAYERS

Some roses growing on their own roots produce *suckers* at the base of the plant. The suckers have roots of their own, so you can dig them up in early spring (keeping plenty of soil around the roots) and plant them elsewhere just as you would a new rose.

Layers are almost as easy as suckers, but you need a rose that produces long, flexible canes. In spring, select a mature cane growing close to the ground, and bend it to touch the soil. Loosen the soil there, and work in a shovelful of compost.

Long, flexible canes make layering this 'Mme. Isaac Pereire' rose easy.

With a sharp knife, slice along the underside of the cane where it will touch the ground; make the cut about 3 inches long and no deeper than halfway through the cane. Dust the cut with rooting hormone, and insert a pebble to hold it open.

Bury the cut section, and hold it down with a piece of wire. Firm the soil around it, keep the soil moist, and, when you are sure roots have formed (a few months to a year), cut the new plant free from the parent plant. Dig it up, keeping plenty of soil around the roots, and plant it in its new location.

A Rose Gardening Calendar

Roses thrive on attention, at least a little in every season. If you care for them at the proper time, you'll be rewarded—they'll grow strong and healthy, and you'll be able to sit down and enjoy them.

SPRING

- Finish planting new bare-root roses; plant new container-grown roses (see pages 32–35).
- Plant roses into display pots (see pages 36–37).
- Start a new rose by digging up and replanting a sucker from an own-root rose, or by layering a long, flexible cane (see page 53).
- Apply fertilizer to give roses a boost for the coming growing season (see pages 40–41).
- Spread an organic mulch around roses; in cold-winter climates wait until the soil has warmed (see page 38).
- Check the soil for moisture (see page 38); if necessary, begin watering deeply to keep the root zone moist.
- Start inspecting your roses frequently for pests and diseases (see pages 46–49); aphids are common on new spring growth.
- Remove and discard suckers from budded roses (see page 60).
- To propagate, take rose cuttings from shoots that have just flowered (see page 52).
- Fertilize roses after the first round of spring bloom (see pages 40–41).
- After they have flowered, prune climbing roses, ramblers, shrub roses, and species roses that flower only in spring (see pages 58–65).

SUMMER

- Check the soil for moisture (see page 38); if necessary, water more often to keep the root zone moist. Check roses in pots daily in hot or windy weather (see page 39).
- Check the mulch; replenish it if necessary, to keep the layer 2 to 3 inches thick.
- Remove weeds as they appear. Try not to disturb the mulch.
- Train and tie in the long new shoots of climbers.
- Deadhead repeat-flowering roses to encourage the next cycle of blooms.
- Prune away weak, broken, or diseased stems.

- Disbud grandifloras and floribundas to make a more impressive flower display.
- Continue applying fertilizer to repeat-flowering roses through the summer; in cold-winter climates, stop fertilizing 6 weeks before the expected frost date (see page 41).
- Keep the rose garden clean: remove fallen leaves, petals, and debris.
- Continue to watch for pests and diseases.
- Visit rose gardens and rose nurseries to study new varieties and plant combinations.

FALL

- Check soil moisture (see page 38); reduce the amount of irrigation or the number of applications if appropriate, but keep the entire root zone moist as plants prepare for dormancy.
- In cold-winter regions, drain underground sprinkler irrigation systems before the first freeze; drain above-ground drip lines,

Controlling Weeds

Spreading a thick layer of mulch (see page 38) around your roses in spring and keeping it topped up throughout the season are good strategies for controlling weeds. Laying landscape fabric is another option, but you'll need to put mulch on top of it so it doesn't show.

Pull weeds as they appear. If you like to use a hoe, hoe shallowly or you may damage the rose roots. Herbicides must be used with extreme caution around roses; if spray touches the rose foliage, it will kill the leaves and possibly the whole plant (see page 43).

and consider taking them up and storing them indoors until spring.

■ To grow new roses from seed (see page 53), collect hips when they change color; don't wait until they shrivel.

■ Assess the performance of your roses this year. Decide which, if any, need to be replaced. Place your rose order early.

■ If you are planning to plant new roses, check the soil pH and drainage, and get the ground ready (see pages 30–31). In most climates, it's best to delay planting until early spring (see page 32).

■ In cold-winter climates, protect roses against winter freeze damage (see pages 50–51).

WINTER

■ Check soil moisture (see page 38); continue watering while the soil is not frozen.

DISBUDDING CLUSTER ROSES

Many roses, particularly grandi-floras and floribundas, produce flowers in clusters or sprays, the central flower opening first, followed by the others. To get a bigger, better, and neater display, pinch out the central bud, so it doesn't hold back the opening of the others.

Deadheading

Deadheading your roses—cutting off the flowers when they fade—keeps the garden looking fresh and attractive. If you have repeat-flowering roses, it will also give you more and big-

ger flowers during the next bloom cycle.

Cut the dead flower, or spray of flowers, back to a healthy leaf with five leaf-lets, on the outside of the bush, two or three leaves down from the flower if the bush is mature and vigorous (remove less stem on a new or struggling bush). A new shoot will grow from the leaf axil.

If you have lots of free-flowering roses and little time for deadheading, you can shear the bushes instead, but they may take longer to bloom again.

■ Clean tools, sharpen pruners, check the expiration dates of pesticides.

■ Plan any new rose beds, checking color combinations and planting distances (see pages 27 and 33).

■ In cold-winter regions, if plants start to heave out of the soil, pack soil around them as best you can.

■ For best selection of new rose plants, order from mail-order catalogs or watch for the arrival of bare-root plants in local nurseries (see page 24).

■ In mild-winter regions, plant new bare-root roses in January and February (see pages 32–35).

■ In cold-winter regions, remove winter protection from roses only at the end of the dormant season, just before pruning (see page 51).

■ As growth buds along the canes begin to swell, prune hybrid teas, miniatures, and varieties of climbers and shrub roses that repeat-bloom (see pages 58–65).

■ After pruning, do a careful winter cleanup, removing prunings, dropped leaves, and old mulch. Then spray plants and soil with horticultural oil and lime-sulfur fungicide to kill any insect eggs and disease spores (see page 46).

CHAPTER THREE

Pruning and Training

ONCE YOU FALL IN LOVE *with your roses, it's irrelevant that roses have grown wild and been beautiful for thousands of years without pruning or training. You want to prune them so that they have a chance to rejuvenate every year and produce a more lovely show. From there, you go on to dreaming how a rose might look trained over a window, its cupped blossoms sagging into view from inside the house. Or perhaps you'd like to try a pillar of roses with the flowers aloft and gay against the sky, or to set a rose loose into a tree so you can witness it making its own wild way through the foliage into the sun. ✿ Pruning and training are fairly simple. Most roses, as you'll find out in this chapter, don't need much pruning. And training can be as easy as pegging a few canes into the ground or tying them to the beams of an arbor.*

'Coral Dawn' climbing a rustic log arbor.

Pruning Roses

All roses benefit from annual pruning. You may enjoy pruning each cane with precision pruning shears, or perhaps your instinct is to lop off the top of the bush with hedge shears; sometimes it matters which you do, and sometimes it doesn't. Here's what you should know about pruning different types of roses.

WHY PRUNE?

Pruning allows you to shape your rose bush, and it's good for the plant. With careful pruning, you can make your rose pleasingly symmetrical, or direct it toward an arch or a window, or reduce its size if it has grown out of bounds. Pruning also encourages new growth, promotes large flowers, and keeps a rose healthy.

The benefits of pruning outweigh any consequences of the few mistakes you might make as you learn to prune. So relax, if you are pruning for the first time; you'll be a confident pruner by next year and able to correct any errors.

WHEN TO PRUNE

For *repeat-flowering roses,* the best time to prune is toward the end of the dormant season, when the buds along the canes begin to swell. In mild-winter regions, this can be as early as January; in the coldest-winter areas, April may offer the first opportunity.

In the many areas where chilly, wintry days alternate with more springlike spells during March and April, it's hard to know when to prune. Gardeners in those areas often use one of two indicators: either they prune when forsythia comes into bloom, or they prune about 30 days before the area's last expected killing frost (your local nursery will know when that is).

For *roses that flower only in spring* (mostly old garden roses), pruning at the end of the dormant season cuts away some of that spring's potential flowers. For the most abundant bloom, therefore, delay your major pruning until just after these roses flower. But remove any dead or old, unproductive canes while the plants are dormant and leafless, because it's easier to see what you are doing then.

PRUNING TOOLS

To prune roses well, you need at least two basic tools: sharp pruning shears and a small pruning saw.

The shears can do most of the work, but a pruning saw helps you remove large-diameter old canes and dead wood. Buy hook-and-blade (bypass) shears, the type with two curved blades that cut like scissors, rather than the anvil type, which has one curved and one flat blade that make a snap cut. The hook-and-blade design makes cleaner, closer cuts and is less likely to crush stems than the anvil type.

Two other tools may also be useful, if you have certain types

CLOCKWISE FROM TOP LEFT: *Hook-and-blade pruning shears, pruning saw, hook-and-blade loppers, hedge shears with extra-long handles.*

THINNING, CUTTING BACK

There are two forms of pruning: thinning and cutting back. It's important to know the difference, because they produce quite different results.

THINNING Thinning is removing an entire shoot or cane back to its point of origin. For example, you might cut a spindly shoot back to a strong cane or cut an unproductive old cane back to the base of the plant. These thinning cuts don't stimulate new growth the way cutting back does (see below). Thin to remove dead wood and damaged, diseased, or weak canes; to reduce the size of a bush; and to open up the center of a bush.

CUTTING BACK Cutting back is removing just part of a cane, not all of it as you do in thinning. You cut back to just above a bud, which stimulates buds just below the cut to grow. The immediate result of cutting back is a smaller, more compact bush—but it does not stay that way for long. The cut-back canes soon put out vigorous new growth and produce large flowers. Cutting back is also useful to direct growth: if you want a strong cane to grow over a window or away from the center of the bush, cut it back to just above a bud that is facing in the desired direction.

Shearing is a quick, imprecise form of cutting back. It's particularly suitable for hedges and ground covers.

Slip-on protective sleeves.

of roses. Loppers are helpful for pruning the interiors of large bushes, which may be too congested and thorny to reach comfortably with regular pruning shears. Their long handles also give you more leverage to make clean cuts in thicker canes. Again, choose a hook-and-blade design.

Hedge shears are the best tool for pruning a lot of landscape roses (shrubs, hedges, or ground covers). Consider buying ones with extra-long handles to extend your reach.

Before you start to prune, put on a pair of protective heavy gloves that thorns can't puncture. You might also like to equip yourself with protective arm wear.

Thinning cuts are shown in gray, cutting-back cuts in red.

Right   Wrong   Right   Wrong   Wrong

When you're removing an entire cane (thinning), cut it flush with the bud union or growth from which it sprang. Don't leave a stub, or it will die back, allowing entry to disease.

When you're cutting back a cane, make a slanting cut at approximately a 45° angle. The lowest point should be opposite and slightly higher than the bud; the upper point should be ⅛ to ¼ inch above the bud. If you angle the cut down toward the bud, water will drain into it and might damage it; if you cut too high, the stem may die back and become diseased.

GOOD CUTS

Pruning cuts do no harm if you make them cleanly and in the correct places. However, if you leave behind stubs and crushed or ripped canes, you create new havens for pests and diseases.

Before you start cutting, be sure your tools are sharp and up to the job: pruning shears can usually easily cut canes up to ½ inch thick; for thicker canes, switch to loppers or a saw.

Start the cut in the correct place, not too high and not too low.

CUTS AFTER FROST DAMAGE

In cold-winter climates, frosts may kill part or all of each cane. Cut back past the blackened areas as far as necessary until you reach healthy tissue. You'll know when you get there because the pith, at the center of the cane, will be white, not brown.

WHAT TO DO WITH SUCKERS

On budded plants, a shoot called a *sucker* may grow from below the bud union. Cutting it off won't solve the problem; you'll get new suckers before long. Instead, grasp the sucker and pull it *down* and off the plant. If it originates from below ground, gently remove the soil, track the sucker back to the roots, and pull it off from there.

DON'T PRUNE TOO HARD

Pruning removes some of the reserves of nutrients that are stored in the canes for the next season's growth. When you have the option (when the canes haven't been killed back too far by frost), prune your rose lightly or moderately.

Removing a sucker.

PRUNING HYBRID TEAS, GRANDIFLORAS, FLORIBUNDAS, AND POLYANTHAS

Regardless of where you live, you can follow the two steps below to prune these popular modern roses. Almost all are repeat-flowering, so you prune them at the end of the dormant season, when the buds begin to swell. Before you start, spend a minute studying your bush; notice that the canes are of varying thicknesses, ages, and health.

1 *Thin* the bush: Entirely remove old canes that produced only spindly growth last year. Also remove weak, twiggy branches. Now open up the bush by removing branches that cross through the center. This will give you a vase-shaped plant— slender or fat, depending on your rose's natural habit—without a central tangle of twigs and leaves that can harbor insects and diseases. (Gardeners in very hot climates often just shorten these central branches, rather than removing them, so they will produce leaves to shade the canes.)

2 *Cut back* the remaining stems. In mild-winter regions, reduce the length of the remaining healthy stems by about one third (a little less than that for floribundas and polyanthas). In cold-winter regions, where the canes may be killed back to their protecting mound, you have to cut back more heavily— until you reach white healthy pith. Make slanting cuts (see the previous page) to outward-facing buds, which will help keep the center of the bush open. (If you want to encourage a spreading bush to grow more upright, cut to inward-facing buds.)

Remove the Prunings

When you have finished pruning—either deadheading in summer or the annual pruning during winter or spring—rake up the prunings, and dispose of them. Left in place, they may become a breeding ground for pests and diseases that overwinter in debris. Composting the prunings isn't recommended, because it may not kill the insect eggs and fungal spores. Once you have raked the garden clean after winter pruning, before the plants leaf out, spray your roses with a preventive mix of horticultural oil and lime sulfur.

Raking up debris.

Mystery Bushes

What should you do if you don't know what kind of bush rose you have? Prune it lightly, removing only dead, damaged, diseased, or crossing stems. During the bloom season, compare the flowers to the photographs on pages 74–120, take a bouquet

of flowers to a local rose society meeting, or contact the American Rose Society (see page 125). Once the rose is identified, you can prune it properly when the following pruning season comes around.

Pruning dead wood.

canes (many of the hybrid perpetuals, for example) can be trained in the manner of climbers and pruned the same way as climbers (see pages 64–65). The floribunda shrub roses can be pruned hard, like regular floribundas (see page 61).

Some of the old garden roses—most gallicas, albas, damasks, centifolias, and moss roses—flower only once, in spring, so they should be pruned after flowering. Most of the modern shrub roses and the other old garden roses—most bourbon, china, portland, hybrid musk, and rugosa roses—are repeat-flowering and are pruned at the end of the dormant season, just before new growth begins.

To prune old garden and shrub roses, follow the two steps below.

PRUNING OLD GARDEN ROSES AND SHRUB ROSES

Most old garden roses and shrub roses need only a light annual pruning—provided you've allowed these typically

vigorous roses sufficient space. They are most graceful if you let them grow naturally, with a little shaping as necessary and thinning to take out the old wood.

The roses in these groups that produce long, arching

1 *Thin* the bush. Cut out a few old, woody stems at the base of the bush if the center of the bush is dense and overcrowded. To keep the bush healthy, remove any dead, damaged, or weak canes and any canes rubbing against or crossing one another.

2 *Cut back* the remaining canes lightly, pruning just the tips. If the center of the bush is crowded, shorten the side shoots to outward-facing buds.

PRUNING GROUND COVERS

Ground cover roses need little pruning. Prune the shrubby types the same way you prune shrub roses: remove any dead, damaged, or diseased canes; and open up the center, if it is too dense, by removing woody canes, shortening the laterals, and pruning the tips of the canes.

Keep rambler types in check by cutting back any wayward, overlong stems. To spread the roses over a larger area, peg down the shoots (see pages 70–71) instead of cutting them back.

PRUNING MINIATURE ROSES

The quick way to prune miniature bush-type roses is to take a pair of hedge shears to them, and trim them into a pleasing dome shape. The more precise, finicky method is to prune them as you would hybrid teas and floribundas (see page 61); the bushes will look nicer up close if you prune them carefully like this.

A rangy miniature bush rose before pruning.

After careful pruning it is compact and ready to grow vigorously.

Prune lightly if the bushes are growing and flowering well; if they are rangy—miniatures grown in pots sometimes are—reduce the length of the canes by half or even three-quarters, to encourage bushy, compact, new growth.

Prune miniature ground covers, standards, and climbers as you would their full-size counterparts.

Pruning Rose Hedges

Prune hedges as you would the individual roses in them. Cut back any shoots that depart from the general lines of the hedge, but don't try to force the bush into a formal shape; by nature a rose hedge is informal. To encourage new canes to grow from the bases of the bushes remove some of the old woody canes and apply Epsom salts (see page 40).

'Complicata' hedge.

PRUNING CLIMBING ROSES

A variety of roses climb: true climbers, climbing varieties of bush roses, ramblers, and some shrub roses that get carried away in mild climates. What they all have in common is long, flexible canes that produce most of their flowers along the length of the cane.

The best way to prune a climber depends on whether it repeat-blooms through the summer—most popular climbers do—or blooms only once, in spring. (To prune a rambler, see the next page.) After pruning, train the remaining canes into position (see pages 66–71).

REPEAT-BLOOMING CLIMBERS

After planting, let the rose grow unpruned for 2 to 3 years, which will give it time to become established and build up strength to put out good climbing canes. Remove only dead, damaged, or diseased

GLUE FOR BORERS

It's unnecessary to treat small pruning cuts, but you can seal them with dabs of white glue if you have had cane borers (see page 49). Very large pruning cuts may heal more quickly if you treat them with pruning paint.

shoots during this time. In subsequent years, just before growth begins in spring, follow the steps as shown below.

1 Remove the old and obviously unproductive canes—the ones that produced no strong growth the previous year.

2 On the remaining canes, cut back to two or three buds all the side branches (called *laterals*) that flowered during the last year; this will encourage spectacular new blooms all along the canes.

SPRING-BLOOMING CLIMBERS

Prune just after flowering. To replace old canes with vigorous new ones, thin out the oldest and least vigorous canes. The plant will put out new canes and laterals on the remaining canes to carry next spring's flowers.

PRUNING RAMBLERS

Prune ramblers after they have finished flowering and when new growth has begun. Completely remove canes that have just flowered and show no sign of producing any long, vigorous new shoots. On canes that have flowered and are starting to send out some strong new growth, cut back to the new growth.

PRUNING STANDARD ROSES

Prune standard bush roses as you would a regular bush rose of that type (many are hybrid teas; see page 61), but pay particular attention to shaping the head so that it looks symmetrical and is open at the center. During the growing season, check for and remove any shoots that grow from the trunk.

Weeping standards, which may be created with a rambler or a climbing or ground cover rose, shouldn't be pruned as hard as hybrid teas. For 2 years after planting, simply remove any dead, damaged, or diseased wood, and cut back any weak shoots. In following years, remove some of the old canes—

Pruning Roses in Trees

A fairly restrained climber growing in a small tree may be reachable from a ladder when it's time for deadheading and pruning. A rampant rambler planted beneath a tall tree, however, may quickly escape way over your head to the treetop—and from there to another treetop or your neighbor's roof. If you need to keep it within bounds, remove most of the old canes every year.

Rambler 'Alberic Barbier'.

just one or two each year if the rose is only moderately vigorous; as many as you like if the rose is supervigorous. To complete the pruning, follow the pruning guidelines for the individual rose type.

Shape the head symmetrically.

Pinch off shoots from the trunk.

Training Roses

Roses don't climb naturally, the way ivy and honeysuckle do. You must train them—tie their stems to something—if you want them to grow up a wall or archway or other structure. Perhaps you'd like them to grow along the ground or to form neat, unusual shapes—well, you can train them those ways too.

BENDING CANES FOR MORE FLOWERS

Left to their own devices, the long canes of most climbing roses grow upward, and the buds along the canes don't develop. Most of the leaves and flowers are then at the top of the plant.

To bring the flowers closer to eye level, and increase the number of flowers, train the canes horizontally, or as close to horizontal as they'll go. This encourages the many buds along the canes to grow; a few will develop as *growth laterals,* but most will become *flowering laterals* profuse with blooms.

Some short, stiff-caned climbers (called *pillar-climbers* or *pillar roses*) grow upright and still produce flowering laterals. They are more like narrow shrubs than actual climbers, and the canes don't require bending.

ROSES ON FENCES AND WALLS

For a low fence, select a modest-growing climber or lax shrub rose; a rampant climber is suitable only for a very large wall. You can tie the rose canes directly to a rail fence. On solid fences and walls, you need to install supporting wires or a trellis.

WIRES Screw eyebolts into the fence posts or wall; space them about 4 feet apart. Place the lowest wire 18 inches off the ground and the wires above it 15 inches apart. Leave as much space as you can between the wires and the fence or wall to improve air circulation around the rose and reduce the risk of pests and diseases, such as mildew.

If your surface is stone, concrete, or brick, drill holes for the eyebolts, insert expanding anchors (preferably lead) into the holes, and screw the eyebolts into the anchors.

Thread 14-gauge galvanized wires between the eyebolts, and twist the wires to secure them in place. Tie the rose canes to the wires; don't weave the canes around them.

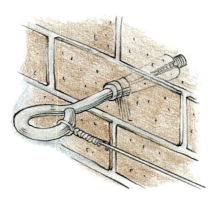

Attaching wires to masonry.

TRELLIS A trellis with an 8- to 12-inch grid is a suitable support for climbing roses. Use wood spacer blocks to keep the trellis at least 4 inches away from the fence or wall, for good air circulation. Because the trellis will be heavy, attach it to the wall framing or to posts, not just to thin siding or fence boards. Use lag screws; on a masonry wall, insert expanding anchors. In very-cold-winter climates, if you plan to tip your climber to protect it (see pages 50–51), avoid weaving the canes through or around the trellis, because they'll be difficult to remove.

Good air circulation.

TRAINING After pruning in spring, allow any new young canes to grow upward; make no attempt to train them. Take the mature canes, last year's growth, bend them from the vertical, and tie them in place.

If the canes are fairly limber, you can angle them outward into horizontal positions; if they are a bit stiffer, you may have to settle for spreading them into a vase outline. In either case, tie the canes into place with their tips pointing downward.

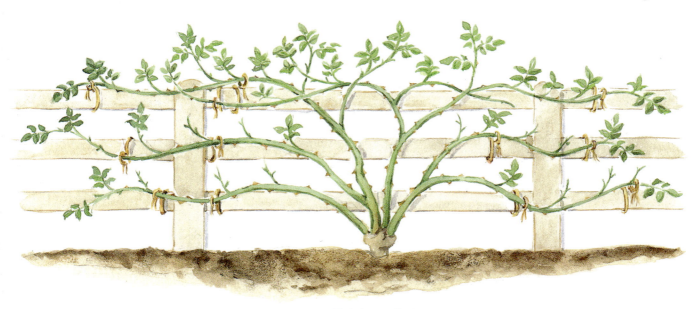

Training a climber.

Follow the same procedure with the mature growth laterals, which will encourage them to produce flowering laterals.

TIPS ON TIES

Avoid using wire or nylon twine to tie rose canes to supports, because it will cut into the canes as they grow. Plastic tape is soft and stretches. You can also use raffia or twine, but you must remember to loosen those ties periodically.

Tie the tape or twine around the support first, and then tie it once again, loosely, around the rose cane.

Tie twice.

Classic Partners: Rose and Clematis

Choose a clematis that flowers at the same time as your rose and that you can prune in the same season. (Clematis are divided into three groups: group 1 clematis are pruned after flowering, at the same time as roses that bloom only once a year; groups 2 and 3 are pruned in early spring, before flowering, the same time as repeat-blooming roses.) Choose a clematis variety with a modest growth habit, not a rampant plant that will overwhelm and perhaps pull down the rose.

Let the rose grow for 2 years to build a framework for the clematis to climb on. Plant the clematis at least 1 foot from the rose, preferably in a place where its roots will be shaded. It will support itself by twining its leaf stalks around the rose stems.

Clematis 'Elsa Spath' (group 2) has a modest growth habit.

ROSES ON ARCHES, ARBORS, AND PERGOLAS

It's easy to grow a rose over an arch, an arbor, or a pergola. First, choose a variety that will grow to a height appropriate for your structure (some climbing hybrid teas reach only 7 feet; some ramblers grow to 30 feet). Plant one rose at the foot of each post, about 15 inches away from it, to allow room for the rose's roots. Then train the roses as follows:

1 Guide the rose canes up the posts. Spiral them around the posts—separately, not as a bunch—to encourage flowering laterals to develop along the canes. Tie the canes to the posts with bands of plastic tape or twine.

2 When the canes reach the tops of the posts, bend them over the structure. For a full effect, train stems along each piece of an arbor or a pergola, the diagonal braces as well as the horizontal beams. Wrapping the canes around the beams, or the top of the arch, also makes the roses fuller. Tie the canes in place regularly during the growing season.

ROSES IN TREES

A climbing rose can support itself in a tree once its long canes, with their hooked thorns, have threaded through the branches. But you'll need to help it scale the trunk.

Plant the rose a few feet from the tree trunk, so it has room to spread its roots. And place it on the side of the tree that faces the prevailing wind, so that the wind will blow the rose stems against and into the tree, instead of away from it. As you plant, tip the rose toward the tree, as you would if you were planting a climbing rose next to a wall (see page 35).

If the rose canes do not reach the tree trunk, place stakes, as

(see page 35)

> ### RAMBLERS VERSUS CLIMBERS
> Ramblers grow fast and are easy to train, because they have lax, pliable stems. But nearly all of them bloom only once, in spring, and they need heavy annual pruning. Climbers generally repeat-bloom through the summer, but they have stiffer canes, which are harder to train.

shown, to guide the rose canes to the tree. Secure the stakes to a band of twine or tape looped around the tree.

As the rose grows, loop twine or plastic tape around the trunk, as shown, to secure the canes. Check at least twice a year that the ties are not cutting into the rose canes or the tree trunk. To increase flowering, spiral the canes around the trunk.

As soon as the rose gets a hold among the tree branches, you can remove the climbing aids.

Guide stakes.

Trunk ties.

Rose Swags for Paths and Boundaries

To make a swag, attach a rope—the thick nautical type—or chain to hang loosely between the tops of two posts. Plant a rose at the base of each post, and train the canes up the posts, securing them to the posts with plastic tape. Then train the canes along the swag to meet midway.

The rose shown here is a wichuraiana hybrid rambler, 'Alberic Barbier'. Wichuraiana hybrids are ideal for swags because they have long, flexible canes and heavy bloom clusters. But usually they flower only once, in spring, and they need retraining every year: At the end of the growing season, untwine the canes, and cut away all but two or three of the strongest new ones on each rose. Train those up the posts, and wind them around the rope or chain, tying them at intervals with tape.

Any climber with fairly limber canes can be grown on a swag. Follow the pruning instructions on page 64, and then train the canes along the swag and tie them in place.

Swags make a beautiful boundary for a rose garden: Install a series of posts, and train the roses in just one direction, toward the next post, except for the rose at the last post, which has to be trained back toward its neighbor. If you don't need to walk under the swag, perhaps loop it a little lower than shown here, so you can smell the roses.

A swag of 'Alberic Barbier'.

ROSES ON TRIPODS AND PYRAMIDS

An open, spreading shrub or small climber, such as a hybrid musk, bourbon, or kordesii climber, is easy to train on a pyramid or tripod. Plant the rose in the center of the structure; if your pyramid or tripod is extra-large, plant a rose inside each corner. Attach the most vigorous canes to the corners. Weave the canes around the structure as they grow, tying in the new growth while it is flexible. Use new canes that grow from the base of the plant to plug any large gaps.

A rose on a tripod.

PEGGING DOWN ROSES

The flexible canes of vigorous shrub, rambler, and hybrid perpetual roses can be bent down and pegged to the ground, for various effects. Make pegs from lengths of wire, forked twigs, or notched or crossed wood stakes.

GROUND COVER ROSES You can peg down the long arching stems of ground cover roses if you want to spread the plants over a larger area, keep them looking prostrate, or increase flowering. Simply bend the stems, lay them along the ground, and peg them in place. (The stems may root where they touch the ground; see page 53 if you'd like to propagate more plants this way.)

Pegged-down ground cover.

Roses on Pillars and Posts

Choose a climbing rose that grows only 8 to 10 feet tall (small shrub climbers, called *pillar roses* are ideal). Plant it about 15 inches away from the foot of the pillar, to allow room for the rose's roots. Wind the canes in a spiral around the pillar; you can run all of them in the same direction or braid them—half clockwise, half counterclockwise—for an attractive pattern.

Consider the best way to tie the canes to the pillar. If your pillar is like the one shown, you can use simple tape ties around its horizontal extensions. If the pillar is a smooth column, you might attach eye hooks to it and tie the canes to those, or you might loop soft green or clear plastic tape around the column to secure the canes. For an elegant pillar or one that is easily damaged, consider installing a slim trellis against one side of it or running wires from the top of the pillar to the ground and attaching the canes to those.

A rose braided on a pole.

Creating a Cascade of Flowers

To encourage a climber to produce a cascade of flowers down to the ground, rather than a cluster all at the top, prune the canes to different heights. Train the mature canes to climb to the tallest point, such as a balcony or the peak of an arbor. Cut back a couple of younger canes to the halfway point, and cut back the very youngest canes to within 2 or 3 feet of the ground.

'Joseph's Coat' in bloom from top to bottom.

SHRUBS AND CLIMBERS Pegging down some of the long stems of vigorous shrub and climbing roses will encourage them to produce more flowers along the stems. It also helps to keep vigorous roses within bounds. Bend the stems carefully, so they don't snap. Ask someone to hold the stem as you peg it; it may hurt you if it flies loose.

Partially pegged-down shrub against a wall.

Partially pegged-down shrub freestanding.

CHAPTER FOUR

More than 390 Recommended Roses

YOUR DREAM ROSE might be an opulent cup of a hundred damask-scented petals delicately tucked and quartered, or a long, elegant hybrid tea bud unfurling to a high-centered blossom. Perhaps it's a sturdy shrub that blooms brightly all summer, resists diseases, and weathers hard winters, or a fragrant wild climbing rose, with hips among the flowers, that reminds you of an old country garden. ❧ All those and more are here, recommended by six rose experts from different regions who have each grown hundreds. They've listed their favorites in every color and rose category, and then each selected a handful to recommend above the others. ❧ Browse this chapter, seeking all the roses in the color you have set your heart on. Or check the varieties listed by the rose expert in your region on pages 121–124. Or just let the images and descriptions here steer you to something new.

Rose blossoms vary not only in color but also in the number and arrangement of their petals and in their scent.

Hybrid Teas and Grandifloras

Hybrid teas and grandifloras are the classic, aristocratic roses with long, stylish pointed buds that spiral open to large blossoms with high centers. Hybrid teas typically carry one blossom at the end of each flowering stem, bloom profusely in spring, and then continue to produce blossoms—either in flushes or continuously—until frosty weather. Their strong, long stems are good for cutting and bringing indoors. Grandifloras are much like hybrid teas but produce small clusters of blossoms as well as individual blooms.

Hybrid teas and grandifloras tend to have an upright, narrow, almost stiff habit. Group three or more together to create a generous, bushy look, unless you choose plants described as bushy. Consider underplanting them with perennials or placing them behind a low hedge to hide their bare ankles—the bases of the canes are usually sparse in foliage. Both types need good conditions and good care. They are not as hardy in cold-winter climates as most shrub roses and species roses, and are generally more susceptible to pests and diseases. Those described as short (or low-growing) are under 3 feet high. Medium are around 4 feet. Tall reach 5 feet or more.

In the listings, AARS means the rose has received the All-America Rose Selections award (see page 26). For some roses, an alternative name is noted in parentheses. For an explanation of plant and flower form terms, see pages 6–7.

Artistry
Hybrid tea; 1998 / From the plump, pointed buds to the broad-petaled open blossoms, the color remains largely unchanged. Mild fragrance. Plenty of large, glossy leaves. Husky, medium tall. AARS.

Abbaye de Cluny
Hybrid tea; 1996 / This Romantica rose, not obviously a hybrid tea, is much admired by Larry Parton, in Spokane, Washington. "My personal favorite of all my 600 roses, this 3-foot variety has huge apricot blooms of old form with a wonderful fragrance. I pick a flower and carry it around with me sometimes." For a list of Parton's recommendations, see page 123.

Bewitched
Hybrid tea; 1967 / Long, stylish-looking buds on long, strong stems open slowly to fragrant "show-rose" flowers with pale petal backs. Good for cutting. Gray-green leaves. Compact plant. Tall. AARS.

Brandy
Hybrid tea; 1981 / From burnt-orange buds, the large, broad-petaled, prettily formed flowers open well in all kinds of weather. Mildly fragrant. Bronzy new leaves. Medium tall. Poor winter hardiness in cold climates. AARS.

Brigadoon
Hybrid tea; 1991 / From bud to open flower, the delicious combination of strawberry and cream constantly changes: pink-blushed, pointed buds unfold to camellia-like, warm dark pink blossoms with creamy recesses. Fragrant. Good disease resistance. Slightly spreading bush. Tall. AARS.

Candelabra
Grandiflora; 1999 / Long, pointed buds in small clusters open to finely formed coral-orange blossoms. Fragrance is slight. Bushy. Medium tall. AARS.

Caribbean
Grandiflora; 1992 / Full, pointed buds in a blend of tangerine and gold spiral open to softer-toned flowers with pointed petal tips. Moderate fragrance. Long stems. Bright green leaves. Vigorous. Medium height. AARS.

Cary Grant
Hybrid tea; 1987 / The name lets you know this rose has class. Long, tapered buds are a vivid reddish orange, washed yellow at the bases. They open to large, full, well-shaped, intensely fragrant flowers. Medium tall.

Chrysler Imperial
Hybrid tea; 1952 / This classic rose has shapely buds, full blossoms, and a rich fragrance. Petals turn purplish red as they age. Excellent cut flower. Bushy. Medium height. Needs a warm-summer climate. AARS. ARS James Alexander Gamble Rose Fragrance Medal.

Crimson Bouquet
Grandiflora; 1999 / Large, pointed maroon buds open to dark garnet-red blossoms with glossy red petal backs. Good for cutting, although only lightly scented. Glossy leaves. Medium tall. AARS.

Crimson Glory
Hybrid tea; 1935 / Large, velvety deep red flowers, powerfully perfumed, open from pointed ultra-dark red buds. Vigorous, bushy, spreading habit. ARS James Alexander Gamble Rose Fragrance Medal.

Also Recommended

Bride's Dream
Hybrid tea; 1985 / Large, very pale pink, full flowers with a pleasing form open from long, pointed, oval buds. The blossoms are borne singly and are slightly fragrant. Matte medium green leaves. Tall.

Chris Evert
Hybrid tea; 1996 / Finely formed orange-yellow blossoms are finished with red at the tips and have a lighter red blush on the petal backs. Moderately fragrant. Medium height.

Classic Touch
Hybrid tea; 1991 / Large light pink flowers are beautifully formed and slightly fragrant. A sport of 'Touch of Class' (page 85). Tolerates humidity well. Tall.

Crystalline

Hybrid tea; 1987 / Once a greenhouse rose grown for cut flowers, this variety has "escaped" to the garden, where it provides long-stemmed, fragrant flowers with the elegance of fine crystal. Tapered, pointed buds open to full, shapely flowers. Tall.

Desert Peace

Hybrid tea; 1992 / This is a descendant of 'Peace' (page 82) with intensified color. Buds are more slender and pointed than those of 'Peace', and flowers are not as full. Light fragrance. Glossy leaves. Medium tall.

Dainty Bess

Hybrid tea; 1925 / Russ Bowermaster, from Florida, recommends this rose highly for its "marvelous, spicy aroma. Prune it lightly, and it will keep producing blooms all year; unlike many other singles, it does not seem to mind the heat of Florida's west coast." Also tolerates cool summers well. Medium tall. For a list of Bowermaster's recommendations, see page 122.

Double Delight

Hybrid tea; 1977 / These blooms have a delightful fragrance. The red edges increase with heat and the petal's age. Glossy leaves; susceptible to mildew. Medium height. Poor winter hardiness in cold climates. AARS. ARS James Alexander Gamble Rose Fragrance Medal. World Rose Hall of Fame.

Dublin

Hybrid tea; 1982 / The large, classic hybrid tea blooms are borne mostly singly on long, strong stems, which are great for cutting. Performs best in warm climates. Notable raspberry scent. Medium height.

Earth Song

Grandiflora; 1975 / Another popular Buck hybrid (see 'Aunt Honey', page 86), this rose produces long, urn-shaped buds that open to large, cupped, moderately fragrant flowers, which turn a lighter pink as they age. Good disease resistance and winter hardiness. Bushy. Medium tall.

Fame!

Grandiflora; 1998 / Small clusters of large, oval buds open to slightly fragrant, camellia-like blossoms of a dark electric pink, a color impossible to ignore. Extremely robust; tall. AARS.

Elina

Hybrid tea; 1984 / Renowned for its color, elegance, bushy habit, and success in virtually all rose-growing regions, this medium-tall rose is one of Peter Schneider's favorites: "Elina is the greatest hybrid tea I have found for growing in Ohio. Its large, perfect, lemon-yellow blooms appear in profusion all year long on top of a vigorous, trouble-free bush." Light fragrance. For a list of Schneider's recommendations, see page 122.

Fragrant Cloud

Hybrid tea; 1967 / Scarlet-orange buds unfurl to paler flowers with a delightful form and fragrance. Profusely flowering. Glossy leaves. Bushy. Medium height. ARS James Alexander Gamble Rose Fragrance Medal. World Rose Hall of Fame. Peggy Van Allen, in the Northwest, recommends it highly: "'Fragrant Cloud' has always been my favorite. It has intense fragrance and color." For a list of Van Allen's recommendations, see page 123.

Folklore

Hybrid tea; 1977 / A child of 'Fragrant Cloud' (above on this page), this rose has a beautiful form and is intensely fragrant. Vigorous. Tall. Can be grown as a climber.

Glowing Peace

Grandiflora; 2001 / This recent, award-winning grandchild of 'Peace' (page 82) bears golden yellow blossoms suffused with orange. The blooms appear in small clusters and are lightly fragrant. Glossy leaves; burgundy fall color. Bushy. Medium height. AARS.

Gold Medal

Grandiflora; 1982 / Great vigor and good health are among this rose's winning traits. Small clusters of long, oval, golden yellow buds—sometimes tinged with pink or orange—unfurl to large, full, lightly fragrant blossoms. Very tall.

Also Recommended

Gemini

Hybrid tea; 2000 / Oval, pointed, creamy buds tinged with coral-pink open to large, perfectly formed, lightly fragrant flowers, with pink petal edges. As the flowers age, the pink spreads through the petals. Glossy leaves. Tall. AARS.

Heart O' Gold

Grandiflora; 1997 / Large, well-formed yellow flowers have gold centers and cerise-pink edges. The pink spreads over the petals as they age. Carried in large clusters. Strong fragrance. Vigorous. Tall.

Heirloom
Hybrid tea; 1972 / Oval, long, pointed, deep lilac to purple buds open to full, deliciously fragrant flowers in a rare color. Vigorous. Medium tall.

Honor
Hybrid tea; 1980 / Satiny white buds slowly unfurl to really large, long-lasting blossoms. The flowers are lightly scented and only moderately full. Leathery, olive-green leaves; good disease resistance. Tall. AARS.

Ingrid Bergman
Hybrid tea; 1984 / From the shapely, oval buds to the wonderfully formed open flowers, the color remains: a solid rich red with no fading or bluing. Slight fragrance. Good disease resistance. Tolerates cool summers well. Bushy. Medium height or a bit shorter. World Rose Hall of Fame.

John F. Kennedy
Hybrid tea; 1965 / Long, classically tapered buds (often tinged with green) slowly spiral open to form full, notably fragrant, pristine flowers of great size. Flowers have the best form in warm regions. Medium tall.

Joyfulness
Hybrid tea; 1984 / The classic shapeliness of the large blossoms is much admired, as is the changing blend of colors. Mild fragrance. Good for cutting. Bushy. Medium height.

Just Joey
Hybrid tea; 1972 / Here's a pleasing medley of soft warm tones. From attractive buff-orange buds come moderately full, highly fragrant, ruffled flowers that soften to apricot shades. Bushy. Medium height. Good disease resistance. Tolerates humidity well. World Rose Hall of Fame.

King's Ransom
Hybrid tea; 1961 / Long buds of classic hybrid tea shape open to large, full flowers with an unfading chrome-yellow color and a pronounced sweet scent. Glossy leaves. Medium tall. AARS.

Kordes' Perfecta
Hybrid tea; 1957 / Pointed buds of pink-edged cream are huge and flawless; when conditions are right, they spiral open to breathtaking fully double, intensely fragrant flowers. Does best with a little shade (especially in hot-summer regions). Leaves are bronzy when new. Vigorous. Tall.

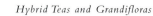

Louise Estes
Hybrid tea; 1991 / Pointed buds open to nicely formed, moderately fragrant pink blossoms with white petal backs. Tolerates heat well. Medium tall.

Love
Grandiflora; 1980 / Brilliant red petals with silvery white backs unfold from beautifully pointed buds. Half-open blooms show red and white, while fully open ones look entirely red. Light scent. Tolerates cool summers well. Somewhat spreading habit. Medium height. AARS.

Jardins de Bagatelle
Hybrid tea; 1986 / A favorite of Michael Ruggiero's, at the New York Botanical Garden: "It produces a multitude of blooms with over 40 petals, over a long season, above distinctive blue-green, disease-resistant foliage. The strong perfume is reminiscent of the old garden roses. Exceptionally winter hardy (with protection) for a hybrid tea rose." Medium height. For a list of Ruggiero's recommendations, see page 121.

Love and Peace
Hybrid tea; 2001 / Another award-winning child of 'Peace' (page 82), this soft yellow rose blushed with pink has a perfect high-centered, spiral form. Blossoms are large, but only mildly fragrant. Glossy leaves. Bushy. Medium tall. AARS.

Marco Polo
Hybrid tea; 1994 / Moderately fragrant, unfading yellow blossoms are carried mostly singly on a vigorous bush. Long stems, good for cutting. Tall.

Also Recommended

Lady X
Hybrid tea; 1965 / Large, double, lavender-pink flowers have only a mild fragrance but are greatly admired for their perfect form. Vigorous. Tall.

Lagerfeld
Grandiflora; 1986 / Medium-size, pointed buds of classic hybrid tea shape swirl open to form small clusters of subtly elegant silvery lavender blooms. Intensely fragrant. Long stems, good for cutting. Matte, medium green leaves; susceptible to mildew. Vigorous, tall.

Lasting Peace
Grandiflora; 1997 / This variety has orange-red buds that unfurl into coral-orange blooms. Mild fragrance. Glossy leaves. Medium tall.

Leonidas
Hybrid tea; 1995 / Blossoms are a striking color for a rose: cinnamon-orange, from ochre buds. Lightly fragrant. Medium height.

Loving Memory
Hybrid tea; 1983 / Attractive buds open slowly to large red blossoms with a slight fragrance. Good disease resistance and surprising winter hardiness for a hybrid tea. Medium tall.

Marijke Koopman
Hybrid tea; 1979 / Lightly fragrant, shapely blossoms in a deep, satiny pink, open from long, pointed buds, usually in small clusters. Vigorous. Medium-tall.

Michelangelo
Hybrid tea; 1997 / This richly colored and perfumed, antique-looking rose is one of the Romantica roses from France. Grows vigorously and quite tall, like a shrub, which is how it is sometimes classified.

Midas Touch
Hybrid tea; 1992 / The blooms glow like beacons in the garden. Pointed buds open to moderately full flowers with jauntily waved petal edges; the blossoms hold their color until the petals fall. Moderate fragrance. Bushy. Tolerates heat well. Medium height. AARS.

Mister Lincoln
Hybrid tea; 1964 / Long, lovely buds open to very full, long-stemmed flowers in a completely satisfying rich red. Powerful fragrance. Glossy leaves, somewhat susceptible to mildew. Good for cutting. Tolerates heat well, and has good winter hardiness for a hybrid tea. Tall. AARS.

Mon Cheri
Hybrid tea; 1981 / The combination of vivid pink and glowing red is almost too bright to look at. Soft pink buds open to very full, lightly fragrant blossoms that turn velvety red wherever sun strikes the petals. Medium height. AARS.

Moonstone
Hybrid tea; 1998 / Very large, beautifully formed ivory-white blossoms are edged delicately with pink. Slight scent. Long stems, good for cutting. Tolerates humidity well. Medium height.

Mrs. Oakley Fisher
Hybrid tea; 1921 / This dainty single rose with bright stamens ranges in color from pale yellow to almost orange (the color is richest in cool weather). Fragrance also varies, from light to strong, so select a plant in flower. Bronzy green glossy foliage. Medium height.

Mt. Hood
Hybrid tea; 1998 / Clusters of pointed buds open to full-petaled, fragrant blossoms. Flowers almost continuously. Glossy leaves. Medium tall. AARS.

Natasha Monet
Hybrid tea; 1993 / The pale lilac beautifully formed blossoms have the most color during cool weather; in hot climates, they may fade to white. Little if any fragrance. Good for cutting. Bushy. Tall.

New Zealand
Hybrid tea; 1989 / Large, wonderfully formed, soft–colored blossoms release a strong honeysuckle scent. Blooms best in cool climates. Good for cutting. Medium height.

Octoberfest
Grandiflora; 1998 / A blend of red, pink, orange, and yellow, this rose has a pleasing flower shape and a slight scent. Glossy leaves; reddish when young. Tall.

Oklahoma
Hybrid tea; 1964 / Inky black buds open to very large, rather globular, dusky red flowers that remain beautiful when fully open; an intense perfume adds to their appeal. Flowers are not at their best in cool, foggy regions. Winter hardiness is good for a hybrid tea. Vigorous. Bushy. Tall.

Olympiad
Hybrid tea; 1982 / From long buds emerge large, long-lasting, lightly scented flowers that hold their color without turning bluish. Long stems. Grayish green leaves. Good disease resistance. Tolerates both heat and cool summers well. Tall. AARS.

Opening Night
Hybrid tea; 1998 / This offspring of 'Olympiad' (left) has inherited the parent's vigor, long stems, and perfect form (from bud to open blossom)— but the blooms have an even richer color. Slight fragrance. Good disease resistance. Tolerates cool summers well. Medium tall. AARS.

Also Recommended

Mellow Yellow
Hybrid tea; 2001 / Mellow and pale in color it is, but it doesn't fade. Flowers are lightly fragrant, large, plentiful, and borne on long stems. Good for cutting. Medium tall.

Mikado
Hybrid tea; 1987 / A touch of yellow at each petal base enhances the bright cherry color. Urn-shaped, flat-topped buds unfold to full, unfading blossoms with a light fragrance. Glossy leaves. Medium height. AARS.

Moon Shadow
Hybrid tea; 1998 / The full, shapely, intensely fragrant flowers are a rare lavender color and usually grow in small clusters. Glossy leaves. Vigorous. Medium height.

Paradise
Hybrid tea; 1978 / A distinctive and changing color combination: ruby red at first edges the young silvery lavender petals and then spreads over more of the petal surfaces as the flowers age. Shapely buds. Moderate fragrance. Good for cutting. Medium height. AARS.

Piccadilly
Hybrid tea; 1960 / Gold petal bases and reverses flash brilliantly with the scarlet surfaces of the petals. Faintly scented. Glossy leaves. Vigorous. Medium height.

Paris de Yves St. Laurent

Hybrid tea; 1995 / Large, attractively formed flowers release a slight fragrance. Good for cutting. Glossy leaves; disease resistant. Medium height.

Pascali

Hybrid tea; 1963 / This is perhaps the finest white rose for dependable production of good-quality flowers in all climates. Tapered, pointed buds unfold to full, perfectly formed, lightly perfumed flowers. Blooms almost continuously. Tall. AARS. World Rose Hall of Fame.

Peace

Hybrid tea; 1945 / Buds of yellow touched with pink or red unfold into extra-large blossoms with pink-rimmed yellow petals (colors vary depending on the amount of heat and sun). Light scent. Glossy leaves; somewhat susceptible to black spot. Medium height. AARS. World Rose Hall of Fame.

Pink Peace

Hybrid tea; 1959 / Numerous plump oval buds open to large, full, shapely blossoms with a heady fragrance. Susceptible to rust. Good winter hardiness for a hybrid tea. Medium height.

Pristine

Hybrid tea; 1978 / This delicate confection of a blossom comes on a plant that is anything but delicate: it's medium tall and spreading, with oversized leaves. Buds are long, oval, pink blushed; they open quickly to full, long-lasting, lightly fragrant flowers.

Proud Land

Hybrid tea; 1969 / Full-petaled, velvety bright blossoms offer a heavy, pervasive perfume. The buds are long, pointed, and produced almost continuously on long stems. Tolerates heat well. Medium height.

Queen Elizabeth

Grandiflora; 1954 / Small clusters of medium-size, radiant pink blooms develop from attractive, pointed buds. Fragrance is mild. Glossy leaves. Tolerates cool summers well. Extremely vigorous and tall; can be used for hedges and background planting. AARS. World Rose Hall of Fame.

Rio Samba

Hybrid tea; 1991 / Pointed buds and moderately full open flowers are a little small for a hybrid tea, but the color makes up for the size. Blooms come both singly and in small clusters. Colors are best in cool climates. Slight fragrance. Bushy. Medium height. AARS.

Secret

Hybrid tea; 1992 / The secret is a sweet-spicy perfume. Lovely pointed, oval buds are a pastel medley of cream, white, and pink; they unfurl to full, shapely blossoms in which the darkest pink tones are brushed on the petal margins. Plum-brown new leaves. Good for cutting. Medium height. AARS.

Signature

Hybrid tea; 1996 / Elegant red buds open to reveal satiny pink petals with pointed tips and brushes of cream on their lower parts. Moderately fragrant. Vigorous. Medium tall.

Sheer Bliss

Hybrid tea; 1985 / Kathleen Brenzel, in California, thinks it is well named: "Elegant pointed buds open to such beautifully formed blooms that they look as though crafted from fine porcelain—angular and refined. The creamy blossoms have the pink blush of an English schoolgirl's cheeks in winter—pure perfection." Fragrant flowers. Glossy leaves. Medium height. AARS. For a list of Brenzel's recommendations, see page 124.

Solitude

Grandiflora; 1991 / Despite a somber-sounding name, this is a bright, vibrant rose. Fully double, large blooms with lightly scalloped petal margins open from small clusters of plump buds that show golden highlights on the petal backs. Lightly fragrant. Vigorous. Medium tall. AARS.

St. Patrick

Hybrid tea; 1996 / Shapely buds slowly spiral open to golden yellow blooms in cool weather, lovely yellow-green ones (hence the name) only when it's hot. Slight fragrance. Gray-green leaves. Poor winter hardiness in cold climates. Medium height. AARS.

Also Recommended

Portrait

Hybrid tea; 1971 / Very shapely blossoms blend two shades: light pink on the petal edges, dark pink in the center. Very fragrant. Glossy leaves. Medium tall. AARS.

Precious Platinum

Hybrid tea; 1974 / Admired for brilliant red color that doesn't fade, vigorous growth, and good disease resistance, this rose lacks only one quality—lots of fragrance. Medium tall.

Rouge Royal

Hybrid tea; 2002 / A recently introduced Romantica rose, with the old-fashioned character and sweet fragrance the Romanticas are known for. The large, quartered blossoms are bright raspberry red. To 4 feet tall.

Stainless Steel

Hybrid tea; 1991 / An improved descendant of 'Sterling Silver' and as classy as its predecessor. Elegantly tapered silvery lavender buds unfold to large, moderately full flowers with a noteworthy perfume. Vigorous. Tall.

Stephens' Big Purple

Hybrid tea; 1985 / Large, intensely perfumed flowers of deepest, darkest purple make this a winner. The buds open slowly. Tolerates cool summers well. Tall.

Tequila Sunrise
Hybrid tea; 1988 / Oval buds open slowly to lightly fragrant cupped blossoms of dazzling yellow petals edged with scarlet. Borne singly and in clusters. Bushy. Medium height.

The McCartney Rose
Hybrid tea; 1995 / Large, long buds open to big, full, high-centered blossoms that become cupped as they age. Named after the ex-Beatle. Very fragrant. Bushy. Medium height.

Sunset Celebration
Hybrid tea; 1998 / This festival of sunset tones celebrates the centennial of *Sunset* magazine. The shapely, full flowers open from long, tapered buds. Moderately fragrant. Tolerates cool summers well. Medium height. AARS. Peggy Van Allen, in the Northwest, recommends it highly: "This rose is always in bloom; as soon as the old blooms fall, new buds are forming." For a list of Van Allen's recommendations, see page 123.

Tiffany
Hybrid tea; 1954 / Large, long buds, as perfect as finely cut jewels, open to moderately full flowers with an intense, fruity fragrance. Susceptible to powdery mildew. Tall. AARS. ARS James Alexander Gamble Rose Fragrance Medal.

Timeless
Hybrid tea; 1997 / Long, tapered buds open slowly to large, moderately full blossoms, which are long-lasting and hold their vibrant, even color from start to finish. Mild fragrance. Good disease resistance. Somewhat spreading habit. Medium height. AARS.

Toulouse-Lautrec
Hybrid tea; 1994 / Delicate tucked and ruffled petals give this rose an antique look, but it's a contemporary Romantica introduction from France. Tapered buds open into flowers that are almost flat; as the blooms age, the outer petals turn a lighter yellow. Fragrance varies. Medium height.

Tournament of Roses
Grandiflora; 1988 / Both the oval buds and the symmetrical, camellia-like open flowers display two shades of pink: dark coral on the petal backs, warm light pink on the upper surfaces. Blooms profusely. Mild fragrance. Glossy leaves; good disease resistance. Vigorous. Medium height. AARS.

Tropicana

Hybrid tea; 1960 / Pointed buds unfold into full, rather cupped flowers with a sweet fragrance. Matte green leaves; susceptible to mildew. Good for cutting. Vigorous, somewhat spreading plant. Tall. AARS.

Uncle Joe (Toro)

Hybrid tea; 1972 / Big is the word for this rose. Long, pointed, oval buds on long stems open slowly to large, full, shapely, moderately fragrant blossoms. Flowers open best where nights are warm. Good winter hardiness for a hybrid tea. Tall.

Touch of Class

Hybrid tea; 1984 / Elegant tapered buds open to large, moderately full, beautifully formed flowers, which are good for cutting. Russ Bowermaster, of Florida, highly recommends this rose: "There is little fragrance, but the foliage is attractive and it resists black spot, which is a distinct advantage in this climate." Bushy. Tall. AARS. For a list of Bowermaster's recommendations, see page 122.

Voodoo

Hybrid tea; 1984 / Dark buds open to large, heavily perfumed flowers that soften in color to yellow and peach shades, then finally fade to pink. Glossy, dark, bronze-green leaves. Tall. AARS.

White Lightnin'

Grandiflora; 1980 / Ruffled petals give the full, intensely citrus-scented blossoms a distinct personality. Glossy bright green leaves. Flowers almost continuously. Bushy. Medium height. AARS.

Yves Piaget

Hybrid tea; 1985 / Fat, pointed buds unfold to deeply cupped, peony-like blossoms with frilly petals and a rich fragrance. Flowers are very large, up to 6 inches across, and produced in abundance. A Romantica rose. To 5 feet tall.

Also Recommended

Traviata

Hybrid tea; 1998 / This dark red Romantica rose has about 100 petals tucked and quartered into each very full bloom. Fragrance is only light. Good for cutting. Disease resistant. Medium height.

Vanilla Perfume

Hybrid tea; 1999 / Smelling sweetly of vanilla, the large, perfectly formed, light cream and apricot blossoms appear singly or in small clusters. Tall.

Veterans' Honor

Hybrid tea; 1999 / Large, shapely, velvety, dark red blossoms give off a light to moderate raspberry scent. Most grow singly on long stems. Part of the proceeds from this rose go to the Department of Veterans Affairs. Medium tall.

Landscape Roses

Landscape roses are flowering shrubs used in borders, as hedges and ground covers, and as background plantings. These roses can be quite trouble-free, and many are hardy in cold-winter climates. New hybridizing programs have produced notably lovely shrubs with striking or sumptuous colors; some are very fragrant. The roses listed here are repeat-flowering (unless otherwise noted).

Landscape roses are commonly divided into the following classes: *English roses,* produced by David Austin, combine the character of old European roses with modern colors and repeat-bloom; many can be grown as small climbers in mild-winter areas, where they reach maximum size. Most *hybrid rugosa roses* are as tough as the *Rosa rugosa* parent (see page 106), with excellent disease resistance and cold tolerance. They have distinctive rugosa foliage, and many form large, round hips. The original *floribunda roses* were as bushy, vigorous, and profuse in bloom as polyanthas, with the color range and flower form of hybrid teas. Today's floribundas range from 2½ to 4 feet tall, and some bear large clusters of rather informal flowers. *Ground cover roses* are low-growing; their canes spread to about three times the plant's height, making an undulating carpet of color. *Hybrid musk roses* typically are vigorous, lax shrubs, with clusters of blossoms; the larger ones can be grown as small climbers in mild climates. This group is notably disease resistant. Most perform well in partial shade as well as full sun. *Polyantha roses* are short and bushy, with large clusters of small blossoms. *Shrub roses,* as an official class, contains English roses, ground cover roses, and roses that fit into no other class. The new Generosa roses and Romantica roses are classified mostly as shrubs; a few are hybrid teas (featured on pages 74–85). The Buck hybrids are bred for cold-winter areas.

In the listings, AARS means that the rose has received the All-America Rose Selections award (see page 26). For some roses, an alternative name is noted in parentheses. For an explanation of plant and flower form terms, see pages 6–7.

Abraham Darby
English rose; 1985 / Apricot, peach, gold, and cream mingle in an always lovely combination in these large, extremely full, cupped, fragrant blossoms. Flowers are abundant and carried in small clusters. A spreading, arching shrub (to about 10 feet) or a modest climber. Large thorns.

All That Jazz
Shrub; 1991 / This vigorous, stiff, bushy shrub grows to about 5 feet tall and has the look of an oversized floribunda. Large clusters of moderately scented blossoms. Plentiful, high-gloss, disease-resistant foliage. AARS.

Aunt Honey
Shrub; 1984 / Larry Parton, in Spokane, Washington, says: "I love many of the Dr. Griffith Buck roses because they are hardy in USDA zone 5 (−20°F/−29°C) and have interesting colors. 'Aunt Honey' and 'Earth Song' [page 76] are prolific and awesome. For gardeners who want reliable, easy-care beauty, these roses are the best." Moderately fragrant. Bushy, to 5 feet tall. For a list of Parton's recommendations, see page 123.

Angel Face
Floribunda; 1968 / Rose and red tints enliven these ruffled, very full, very fragrant lavender blossoms, borne in clusters on a low, spreading plant that blooms heavily. Bronze-tinted leaves. The climbing sport grows to about 10 feet. AARS.

Anthony Meilland
Floribunda; 1994 / Large, lightly fragrant blossoms are held in small clusters. Bush flowers almost continuously. Has a rounded habit, reaching about 5 feet tall.

Apricot Nectar
Floribunda; 1965 / Intensely fragrant, large flowers blushed delicately with apricot, pink, and yellow make this a favorite floribunda. Flowers appear in tight clusters and are long-lasting. To 4 feet tall. AARS.

Autumn Sunset
Shrub; 1986 / Large clusters of pointed buds open to loosely cupped apricot blooms with touches of orange, gold, and peach. Color is best in cool weather. Strongly fragrant. Orange hips in fall. A tall shrub or a moderate climber (to about 12 feet).

Ballerina
Hybrid musk; 1937 / Single, small flowers with the airy charm of dogwood or apple blossoms are carried in giant, domed clusters. Only lightly fragrant. Dense, glossy foliage. Tiny orange-red hips. Tolerates cool summers well. Rounded shrub, to about 5 feet tall.

Belle Story
English rose; 1984 / Shell-like petals unfold around a central tuft of stamens, giving each large bloom the look of a peony. Borne in small clusters, the blossoms appear throughout the growing season and have an unusual fragrance: some say anise; others myrrh. Vigorous, to 4 feet tall.

Betty Boop
Floribunda; 1999 / These bold cherry-red, white, and yellow blossoms, with gold stamens at the center, begin as ivory buds tinged with red. Flowers almost continuously. Moderate fragrance. Glossy leaves are reddish when new. Bushy, to about 4 feet tall and wide. AARS.

Betty Prior
Floribunda; 1935 / Here is all the charm of a wild rose and much of the vigor as well. Red buds open to blossoms that resemble dogwood blooms in size and shape. Lightly fragrant. Blooms almost continuously. Tough, disease resistant, and cold tolerant. To 6 feet tall and wide.

Blanc Double de Coubert
Hybrid rugosa; 1892 / Pointed buds surrounded by elongated sepals flare open to highly fragrant, fairly full but loose blossoms. Leathery, disease-resistant rugosa foliage colors well in fall. Orange hips. Spreads by suckers. Good winter hardiness. Vigorous. Reaches about 6 feet tall.

Blueberry Hill
Floribunda; 1999 / Plump, pointed, dark lilac buds open to large, fragrant, clear lilac flowers with a center of golden stamens. Flowers are carried in small clusters. Glossy leaves. Good disease resistance. Rounded bush, to 4 feet tall and wide.

Buffalo Gal
Hybrid rugosa; 1989 / Michael Ruggiero, at the New York Botanical Garden, chose this as one of his five favorite roses: "It has larger flowers than other rugosas. Its clean rugosa leaves, great fragrance, large red hips, rebloom, and disease resistance make this an easy-to-grow and fabulous rose." To 4 feet tall. For a list of Ruggiero's recommendations, see page 121.

Bonica
Shrub; 1985 / Arching canes form a mounding, spreading shrub to about 5 feet high, decked out in dark, glossy leaves and large flower clusters. Good disease resistance. Faint fragrance. Bright orange hips. Makes a nice hedge. AARS.

Buff Beauty
Hybrid musk; 1939 / Small clusters of very full, shapely, fragrant flowers open a glowing golden apricot, then fade to creamy buff. New foliage is a plum-bronze color. An arching, 6- to 8-foot shrub or small climber. Tolerates humidity well.

Cardinal Hume
Shrub; 1984 / Pointed buds unfurl to antique-looking cupped flowers with a moderate fragrance. Spreading form, to 5 feet tall and a little wider.

Carefree Delight
Shrub; 1993 / This mounding, spreading plant is densely covered in small, dark leaves and reaches about 4 feet high. From spring to autumn, it's covered in a froth of clustered single blossoms. Little or no fragrance. Excellent disease resistance. Makes a good hedge. AARS.

Carefree Wonder
Shrub; 1990 / There's a lively look to these clustered flowers: the carmine-pink petals are backed in creamy white, with a bit of white infusing the margins as well. Fragrance is slight. Upright (to about 5 feet) and bushy. Excellent disease resistance. Makes a good hedge. AARS.

Champlain
Shrub; 1982 / Informally double blossoms come in floribunda-like clusters on a bushy 3- to 4-foot plant with glossy leaves. Lightly fragrant. One of the Canadian Explorer series, bred to survive southern Canadian winters unprotected.

China Doll
Polyantha; 1946 / Rounded clusters of very full, small flowers may appear in such abundance that the glossy, bright green leaves are almost obscured. Slightly fragrant. Low-growing (reaching just 1½ feet) and nearly thornless. Good disease resistance. Nice for containers.

Country Dancer
Shrub; 1973 / Easy is a common description of this Buck hybrid. It's disease resistant, it flowers almost continuously, its petals drop cleanly when they are done, and it has good winter hardiness. The blossoms fade to light pink with age. Moderate fragrance. About 4 feet tall and wide.

Delicata
Hybrid rugosa; 1898 / The cool pink of the scented, silky-petaled blossoms contrasts well with the dense rugosa foliage. After the flowers fade, you'll get a good crop of bright orange hips. Small for a rugosa, about 3 feet high. Good winter hardiness.

Distant Drums
Shrub; 1985 / This rose has a distinct fragrance and unique colors. Oval, pointed purple buds unfurl to large, slightly ruffled flowers that are peachy bronze in the center and light rosy purple at the petal tips. Upright and bushy, to about 4 feet.

Escapade
Floribunda; 1967 / As charming as wild roses, these delicately colored blossoms appear in profusion in large clusters among glossy leaves. Slight fragrance. Bushy, to 5 feet tall. Makes a fine hedge.

Also Recommended

Arthur Bell
Floribunda; 1965 / The creamy yellow flowers have a strong perfume. Vigorous. Good winter hardiness. To about 4 feet tall.

Charlotte
English rose; 1994 / Cupped, fragrant, soft lemon-and-butter-yellow blooms fade to cream on the outer petals. They are borne in small clusters. To 5 feet tall.

Conrad Ferdinand Meyer
Hybrid rugosa; 1899 / Large, cupped, intensely fragrant silvery pink blossoms. Vigorous and tall (to 10 feet); makes a fine pillar rose, small climber, or tall hedge.

Dr. Jackson
English rose; 1992 / Brilliant scarlet single rose with a tuft of golden stamens. No fragrance. Showy hips. To about 4 feet tall and wide.

Easy Going

Floribunda; 1999 / Larry Parton, in Spokane, Washington, ranks this rose among his favorites: "It really stands out from the crowd because of its productivity and gorgeous form. The foliage is beautiful, too, and the plants take on a nice shape. Even if it didn't bloom, it would be a good landscape bush." Glossy leaves. To about 4 feet tall. For a list of Parton's recommendations, see page 123.

Europeana

Floribunda; 1963 / This lightly fragrant rose is a favorite of Russ Bowermaster's, in Florida: "A dark red floribunda with very attractive foliage and large clusters of flowers. It repeat-blooms quite well and resists most diseases. Ideal for use as a landscape plant." Tolerates heat well. To 3 feet tall. AARS. For a list of Bowermaster's recommendations, see page 122.

Fair Bianca

English rose; 1982 / Its floral perfection elicits comparisons to the damask 'Mme. Hardy' (page 104): the blossoms are flat and circular, their petals packed around a green central eye, their strong myrrh fragrance a delight to the nose. To about 3 feet tall, an English rose for a small space.

First Light

Shrub; 1998 / The parents are 'Ballerina' (page 87) and 'Bonica' (page 88), so it's no wonder the child is outstanding. It produces large clusters of nearly circular, single, fragrant flowers with dark red stamens. The dense, rounded, glossy-leaved bush reaches about 3 feet high and wide. AARS.

Flower Carpet and White Flower Carpet

Ground cover; 1989 / floribunda; 1991 / Low (to about 2 feet) and spreading, these lightly fragrant roses are suited to mass plantings as ground covers but also serve nicely as container plants or border plantings. Foliage is dense and glossy. Both tolerate heat well.

Florence Delattre
Shrub; 1997 / This Generosa rose has a fine, old-fashioned form and a rich perfume. Vigorous, with long arching canes, to about 5 feet tall. Makes a fine pillar rose.

Flutterbye
Shrub; 1996 / Pointed, red-tinged yellow buds open to ruffled, fragrant, single yellow flowers that change to creamy buff, pink, and coral—often within a single cluster. Very glossy, disease-resistant leaves. A fountain-like 6- to 10-foot shrub or small climber in mild climates, a more compact (but still large) shrub elsewhere.

French Lace
Floribunda; 1980 / Strongly recommended by Kathleen Brenzel, in California: "I've grown it in an 18-inch-diameter pot on my patio for years. On bright May days, the blooms look as refreshing as dollops of ice cream." Bushy, about 4 feet tall. Tender; not recommended for cold-winter climates, unless grown as an annual. AARS. For a list of Brenzel's recommendations, see page 124.

Glamis Castle
English rose; 1994 / A cross between 'Graham Thomas' (page 92) and 'Mary Rose' (page 94), this rose has cupped, ruffled blossoms with a strong sweet scent. It's small for an English rose, reaching less than 4 feet.

Golden Celebration
English rose; 1993 / Fat yellow buds touched with red open to large flowers that are cupped at the center but open at the edges. Intensely scented, notched petals. Rounded shrub, grows to 5 feet tall.

Golden Wings
Shrub; 1956 / Large soft-colored petals surround a cluster of bright orange-red stamens. Moderately fragrant flowers are borne in small clusters. Tolerates humidity well. Somewhat rounded, to about 5 feet tall and 4 feet wide.

Also Recommended

Fire Meidiland
Ground cover; 1999 / Fire-truck-red flowers open in small clusters on a fast-growing, sprawling plant (to about 2 feet tall and 4 or 5 feet wide). Glossy, bright leaves. Good disease resistance.

Gingersnap
Floribunda; 1978 / Ruffled, slightly scented, glowing orange petals are packed into very full flowers. Rounded, bushy plant, to about 3 feet tall. New leaves are a deep bronze-purple.

Guy de Maupassant
Floribunda; 1996 / This Romantica rose has old-fashioned form and intense perfume. Pretty pink flowers, each reputedly having about 100 petals. Glossy leaves with good disease resistance. Height varies from 3 to 8 feet.

Graham Thomas
English rose; 1983 /
Modest clusters of plump,
red-tinted yellow buds
open to cupped blossoms
of brightest butter-yellow.
Moderate to strong fra-
grance. Canes may reach
10 feet or more in length.
Can be grown as a
climber in mild-winter
climates; elsewhere, it's a
slender, tall shrub.

Heidelberg
Shrub; 1959 / Clusters of
deep red buds open to
large, lightly scented
crimson flowers with
lighter petal backs.
Vigorous; can be grown
as an upright, bushy
shrub, to about 6 feet tall,
or as a small climber, to
about 8 feet tall. Glossy
leaves. Good disease
resistance.

Hansa
Hybrid rugosa; 1905 / Peggy Van Allen, in the
Northwest, says: "It's my favorite rugosa rose. It has a
great fragrance and color, and you can find buds,
blooms, and hips all at the same time on the bush."
Reaches about 6 feet high and wide; makes a superlative hedge. Yellow fall foliage. Orange-red hips.
Good disease resistance and winter hardiness. For a list
of Van Allen's recommendations, see page 123.

Iceberg
Floribunda; 1958 / Kathleen Brenzel, in California,
advises, "If there ever was a rose to use in a big way—
for example, as a hedge along a picket fence or as rose
trees lining an entry walk—this is it. Blooms come
almost continuously on a disease-resistant plant." To
6 feet tall. Sweet scent. Takes both heat and cool summers. Dense glossy foliage. World Rose Hall of Fame.
For a list of Brenzel's recommendations, see page 124.

Kaleidoscope
Shrub; 1998 / These
ruffled blossoms with a
mild sweet fragrance
move through a series of
interesting colors. The
buds are orange-pink;
the petals open tan and
mauve. Glossy leaves. To
4 feet tall.

Kathleen
Hybrid musk; 1922 /
Reminiscent of apple
blossoms, the single flowers appear in airy, lightly
fragrant clusters that
become sprays of bright
orange hips in fall. Gray-
green leaves. Vigorous,
arching bush to about
6 feet tall; can be trained
as a small climber.

Intrigue

Floribunda; 1982 / Another Kathleen Brenzel favorite: "I can never pass this red-purple beauty without stopping to sniff its heady floral perfume. Its color is rich, too—sumptuous, like a velvet robe." In overall appearance, much like a small hybrid tea. Tolerates cool summers well. Rounded, bushy, to about 3 feet tall. AARS. For a list of Brenzel's recommendations, see page 124.

Knock Out

Shrub; 2000 / This stunningly bright rose is also a hit because of its excellent disease resistance, tolerance of humidity and shade, abundance of flowers into fall, reddish purple fall foliage, and orange-red hips. Mild fragrance. Bushy, to about 3 feet tall and wide. Makes a fine low hedge. AARS.

L. D. Braithwaite

English rose; 1988 / The rich flower color comes from its parent 'The Squire' (page 100); blossom shape and plant quality derive from the other parent, 'Mary Rose' (page 94). The large, fragrant flowers retain their red color without bluing. Prickly canes and stems. Upright to slightly spreading bush, about 5 feet high.

Lilli Marleen

Floribunda; 1959 / Moderately fragrant, intensely red flowers are finely formed. Vigorous. Reaches about 5 feet tall.

Livin' Easy

Floribunda; 1992 / Plentiful, high-gloss foliage would make this an attractive shrub even if it didn't bloom. Add the glowing blossoms and you have a garden beacon throughout the growing season. Rounded bush, about 3 feet tall; good for foreground planting and border hedges. AARS.

Also Recommended

Hunter

Hybrid rugosa; 1961 / Here's a rugosa hybrid with some floribunda genes, hence the crimson-red double blossoms and the handsome leaves without wrinkles. Moderate fragrance. Vigorous. Tolerates humidity well. To about 5 feet tall.

Johann Strauss

Floribunda; 1994 / The large clusters of very full, pink, antique-looking Romantica flowers have a mild lemon verbena scent. Bronze-tinted, disease-resistant leaves. Bushy, 2 to 4 feet tall.

Linda Campbell

Hybrid rugosa; 1990 / The foliage is less textured than that of most rugosa hybrids, and the velvety blossoms are the purest red. Large clusters of blooms. Arching; to 8 feet tall; makes a fine tall hedge.

Love Potion

Floribunda; 1993 / A strong raspberry scent wafts from the large, deep lavender blossoms borne in small clusters. Leaves are shiny. To 5 feet tall.

Magic Blanket

Ground cover; 1999 / From scores of tiny peach-colored buds emerge small white flowers with light yellow centers and gold stamens, which cover the bushes all summer. After flowering, petals drop naturally. To 3 feet tall and 6 feet wide. Light fragrance.

Madison
Shrub; 1998 / One of the Towne and Country landscape roses, 'Madison' produces large clusters of small blossoms on a rounded, compact shrub 2 feet high and wide. Petals drop cleanly, so they don't need dead-heading. Usually massed or used as an edging. Slight fragrance.

Margaret Merril
Floribunda; 1977 / This is a child of the superlative white hybrid tea 'Pascali' (page 82), and it has the same admirable form. Small clusters of pointed, off-white buds open to pure white blooms with ruffled petals and a strong perfume blending citrus and spice. Bushy. To 5 feet tall.

Margo Koster
Polyantha; 1931 / Nearly round buds composed of many shell-like petals unfurl to small, cupped flowers resembling ranunculus blossoms. Blooms come in large clusters. Little if any fragrance. Glossy light green leaves. Twiggy plant, 1½ to 2 feet tall.

Marie Curie
Floribunda; 1996 / This small Romantica rose puts out lots of trusses of lightly scented, ruffled shrimp-pink blossoms. Compact in habit, to about 3 feet tall, it's a handsome old-fashioned-looking variety for a small garden or a container.

Marmalade Skies
Floribunda; 2001 / The blossom clusters appear in abundance all summer. They are good for cutting, but only lightly fragrant. Rounded, bushy habit, to about 3 feet tall and wide. AARS.

Martine Guillot
Shrub; 1996 / A light gardenia scent wafts from these sprays of finely formed, creamy blossoms blushed with soft apricot. They are long-lasting and good for cutting. A Generosa rose. To 6 feet tall and a little wider.

Mary Rose
English rose; 1983 / The broadly cup-shaped, lightly fragrant blossoms have outer petals that reflex to form a circular frame. Flowers almost continuously. Bushy, with prickly stems. Susceptible to powdery mildew. Grows 4 to 6 feet high and wide.

Mme. Plantier
Hybrid alba; 1835 / This graceful, tall, arching plant blooms once, in spring, bearing exquisite, fragrant, 2-inch blossoms that capture the essence of old rose beauty. Plump, red-tinted ivory buds. Nearly thornless. As a shrub it grows to 8 feet tall, but it can also be trained as a small climber.

Molineux
English rose; 1994 / 'Molineux' is smaller than 'Golden Celebration' (page 91), 'Graham Thomas' (page 92), and 'The Pilgrim' (page 100), the other yellow English roses listed. It's nicely delicate in color, too. Strong fragrance. Good disease resistance. Tolerates humidity well. To 4 feet tall.

Morning Has Broken
Shrub; 1996 / A child of 'Graham Thomas' (page 92), this rich yellow rose with gold stamens fades slowly to soft yellow as it ages. Blossoms are carried in small clusters. Little if any fragrance. Smaller than its famous parent—to about 4 feet tall and wide. Tolerates heat well.

Outta the Blue
Shrub; 2001 / Larry Parton, of Spokane, Washington, recommends this rose highly: "It was incredible in my garden last year. The bush itself is wonderful, but the blooms are really eye-catching. The colors are very striking—yet under control." Flowers almost continuously. Fragrant. Varies from 3 to 6 feet tall. For a list of Parton's recommendations, see page 123.

Napa Valley
Shrub; 1995 / This small, mounding shrub in the Towne and Country landscape roses series produces bright red, slightly fragrant blossoms in clusters. Small, glossy leaves; disease resistant. To about 2 feet tall and wide.

Nicole
Floribunda; 1985 / The white petals unfurl from the buds with intense cerise-red on the petal edges; the red may then fade in strong sunlight. Light fragrance. Glossy leaves; good disease resistance. Tolerates heat well. Vigorous, to 5 feet tall or taller.

Oranges 'n' Lemons
Shrub; 1994 / Arching canes form a fountain of dazzling yellow blossoms splashed with orange, from 4 to 10 feet tall. It blooms and holds color best in cool weather. Mild to moderate scent. Red new growth. Good disease resistance. Can be grown as a climber or pillar rose in mild climates.

Also Recommended

Moje Hammarberg
Hybrid rugosa; 1931 / Large, intensely fragrant, reddish violet blossoms are crowned with gold stamens. Showy red hips in fall. Dense, crinkled rugosa leaves. To 5 feet tall and wide.

Mountain Music
Shrub; 1984 / These bright pink-yellow blossoms are speckled sometimes with pink, sometimes with yellow. They appear in large clusters. Moderately fragrant. To 3 feet tall and wide.

Nevada
Shrub/hybrid moyesii; 1927 / Early in spring and again in fall, the canes carry white blossoms all along their length. Little or no scent. Somewhat susceptible to black spot. Spreading habit; reaches about 8 feet tall.

Penelope
Hybrid musk; 1924 / Coral-orange buds in medium-size clusters open to fluffy blossoms that vary from creamy pink or apricot to buff–cream, according to weather and season. Sweet scent. Coral-pink hips. Dense and shrubby, to about 6 feet tall.

Pink Meidiland
Shrub; 1984 / Compared to 'Scarlet Meidiland' (page 97), 'White Meidiland' (page 100), and the others of this group, 'Pink Meidiland' is more of a bushy, upright plant. Little if any fragrance. Somewhat susceptible to black spot. To about 4 feet, with ample foliage; makes a fine hedge.

Paul Bocuse
Shrub; 1997 / Kathleen Brenzel, of California, says: "I love the colors of the sky at sunset and the cupped, many-petaled form of old roses. This Generosa shrub combines them. Rich apricot blooms open in clusters—as many as nine blooms, with several buds fattening between them. The plant is disease resistant, too." Light to moderate fragrance. To about 5 feet tall. For a list of Brenzel's recommendations, see page 124.

Playboy
Floribunda; 1976 / These clustered blossoms bring fiery color into the garden. The yellow centers blend out to orange, and the petals are brushed and infused with red toward the margins. Seductive fragrance. Glossy, disease-resistant leaves. Good winter hardiness. To about 3 feet high.

Playgirl
Floribunda; 1986 / Sprays of single, hot-pink blossoms with pretty yellow stamens are produced abundantly through summer into fall. Fragrance is slight. Tolerates humidity well. Bushy and quite compact, to 4 feet tall at most.

Prairie Sunset
Shrub; 1984 / A Buck rose, bred in Iowa for winter hardiness, 'Prairie Sunset' has large blossoms that blend yellow, pink, and orange. Moderately fragrant. To 4 feet tall.

Prospero
English rose; 1983 / It looks, and is perfumed, like a lovely old gallica rose, but it repeat-blooms like the modern rose it is, and it's small enough to be grown in a container. Fat buds. Ruffled rosettes age to an old-fashioned deep purple. Susceptible to powdery mildew and rust. To 4 feet tall.

Red Ribbons

Ground cover; 1990 / Bright yellow stamens grace the centers of lipstick-red flowers that come in clusters. Slightly scented. Plentiful dark green foliage. Low, spreading plant, to 2 feet tall and 5 feet wide.

Regensburg

Floribunda; 1979 / The pinkish ivory buds give no hint of the blooms to come: striking strawberry-pink flowers with white centers, brushings of white on the petal edges, and nearly white petal backs. Sweet scent. Glossy, disease-resistant leaves. To 2 feet tall. Suitable for a container.

Sally Holmes

Shrub; 1976 / Peggy Van Allen, in the Northwest, lists this rose as a favorite: "This is a beautiful vigorous shrub in our area. It has huge flower heads, some as much as 12 inches in diameter. As the outside blooms fade, the inside buds emerge, so it has a long bloom period." Light fragrance. To 8 feet high; in warm regions, can be trained as a climber. Tolerates light shade. For a list of Van Allen's recommendations, see page 123.

Roseraie de l'Hay

Hybrid rugosa; 1901 / Tapered buds unfold into blowsy, pleasantly spice-scented blossoms that become increasingly purple with age. Densely clothed in apple-green leaves that turn to bronzy yellow in fall. Good disease resistance. Tolerates humidity well. Few hips. To 6 feet tall and wide.

Scarlet Meidiland

Shrub; 1987 / Small, ruffled blossoms in unfading scarlet come in great clusters that can weigh down the branches. Little if any fragrance. Glossy leaves. Grows into a husky, arching mound to about 4 feet high and 6 feet across. Good as a tall ground cover, barrier, or informal hedge.

Also Recommended

Peter Mayle

Shrub; 2001 / A rich old-rose fragrance is released from the large, brilliant fuchsia-pink blossoms. To 6 feet tall.

Prairie Harvest

Shrub; 1985 / A Buck rose with large straw-yellow flowers that are sweetly fragrant. Blooms until frost. Glossy leaves. To 5 feet tall.

Prosperity

Hybrid musk; 1919 / Large clusters of elegant buds flushed with pink open to sweetly fragrant creamy white blossoms with a hint of pink in cool weather or light shade. Glossy leaves. Vigorous. To 5 feet tall and wider. Can be grown as a small climber or pillar rose.

Queen Bee

Shrub; 1984 / Velvety dark red blossoms are large, well-formed, beautifully fragrant, and carried in clusters. A Buck hybrid. To 4 feet tall.

Robusta

Shrub; 1979 / Sturdy and fast-growing, with slightly crinkled leaves, this scarlet rose flowers abundantly into fall. Fragrance varies. Disease resistant. Tolerates humidity well. Makes a fine hedge. To 6 feet tall and wide.

Rugosa Magnifica

Hybrid rugosa; 1905 / Almost-flat, magenta-red blossoms with crowns of gold stamens appear until frost. Strong, spicy fragrance. Orange-red hips. Disease resistant. To 5 feet tall and wide.

Sarah Van Fleet

Hybrid rugosa; 1926 / Michael Ruggiero, at the New York Botanical Garden, says: "Most catalogs list it as growing to 8 feet, but 'Sarah Van Fleet' grows to 10 or 11 feet in my garden and is wider than high. Its double rose-pink flowers are highly perfumed and repeat-flower from late spring until frost. Like most rugosa hybrids, it is very disease resistant." For a list of Ruggiero's recommendations, see page 121.

Scentimental

Floribunda; 1997 / Instantly recognizable, the variably striped and marbled blossoms combine rich red and chalk white. Flower shape—from the plump buds to the open flowers—is attractive as well, and the fragrance is, of course, notable. Rounded habit, to about 3½ feet tall. AARS.

Sea Foam

Shrub; 1964 / A creamy foam of clustered, full, rosette-shaped blossoms billows on a sea of glossy leaves. Faint scent. Lax and spreading, to about 3 feet high and twice as wide; makes fine ground cover or container plant, and can also be grown as a small climber.

Sexy Rexy

Floribunda; 1984 / Peggy Van Allen, in the Northwest, describes this as "A very valiant rose; a flower spray is a bouquet by itself." Peter Schneider, in Ohio, says it "provides as stunning an impact as any floribunda in this climate. Its huge pink trusses will completely hide its foliage in June." Mild fragrance. From 3 to 5 feet tall and wide. For a list of Schneider's and Van Allen's recommendations, see pages 122 and 123.

Simplicity, White Simplicity

Floribundas; 1978, 1991 / Classed as a floribunda but promoted as a shrub, 'Simplicity' is a bushy, 4- to 5-foot plant that is easily maintained as an ever-blooming hedge. Slender, pointed buds in small clusters open to cupped blossoms. Little scent. 'Purple Simplicity', 'Red Simplicity', 'White Simplicity', and 'Yellow Simplicity' are in the same mold as the original pink version.

Sevilliana
Shrub; 1976 / Not to be confused with 'Sevillana' (or 'La Sevillana'), a fiery red floribunda, this rose is a Buck hybrid with fragrant, freckled pink petals around a cluster of golden stamens. To 4 feet tall.

Singin' in the Rain
Floribunda; 1994 / The changeable color is hard to nail down: the blooms have been called golden apricot and russet-orange, often with a brownish cast described as cinnamon. The small clusters of blooms have a sweet scent. Glossy leaves; good disease resistance. To about 5 feet. AARS.

Sunsprite
Floribunda; 1977 / Larry Parton, of Spokane, Washington, thinks highly of this rose: "It is still the best yellow rose in my garden. The deep yellow petals hold their color until they drop." Rich fragrance. Flowers almost continuously. Good winter hardiness and tolerates cool summers well. To about 3 feet tall. ARS James Alexander Gamble Rose Fragrance Medal. For a list of Parton's recommendations, see page 123.

Sir Thomas Lipton
Hybrid rugosa; 1900 / Bushy and bulky (to 8 feet high and wide), this one has plenty of leathery foliage to serve as a backdrop for the well-shaped, highly scented blossoms it bears both individually and in small clusters.

Starry Night
Shrub; 2002 / One of two winners of the prestigious ARS All-America Rose Selections award in 2002, this rose blooms profusely. Large clusters of single bright white blossoms almost cover the bush all summer. No fragrance though. From 3 to 6 feet tall and wide. AARS.

Also Recommended

Scabrosa
Hybrid rugosa; 1950 / Fragrant, slightly crinkly, mauve-pink blossoms are up to 5 inches across. Glossy leaves turn color in fall. Large red hips. Good winter hardiness. To 6 feet tall and can be as wide.

Snow Owl (White Pavement)
Hybrid rugosa; 1989 / Fragrant, cupped, white blossoms are centered with showy bright yellow stamens. Impressive hips. Just 3 to 4 feet tall.

Sun Runner
Ground cover; 1992 / Clusters of little buttercup-yellow blossoms with creamy white edges drop cleanly. Small, bronze-tinted, shiny leaves. Light fragrance.

Sunny June
Shrub; 1952 / Rich yellow, single blossoms with amber stamens open in large clusters into late fall. Light scent. Vigorous. To 8 feet in mild climates; can be a small climber or a pillar rose.

Sweet Inspiration
Floribunda; 1991 / Pink blooms with creamy centers appear almost continuously all summer. Little or no fragrance. To 4 feet tall.

The Dark Lady
English rose; 1994 / This lady, alas, is dark red only in cool temperatures; she fades quickly in the heat. Heady old-rose fragrance. Very full blossoms that may nod. To 5 feet tall and a little wider.

Tamora

English rose; 1992 / Michael Ruggiero, at the New York Botanical Garden, says: "Tamora's flowers are made up of over 40 silky petals in a wonderful mixture of apricot, peach, and orange. It's highly fragrant and low-growing, to about 3½ feet tall and wide, and I've had great success using it as a mass planting but could also see it as a low hedge or ground cover." For a list of Ruggiero's recommendations, see page 121.

Sun Flare

Floribunda; 1981 / Bushy plants, to about 2½ feet high, produce great quantities of shapely, fragrant blossoms. The luminous lemon color is beautifully displayed against the bright green, extra-glossy foliage. The climbing sport is sold as 'Yellow Blaze'; it grows to 14 feet. AARS.

The Fairy

Polyantha; 1932 / The small, full-petaled flowers appear in great profusion into autumn. The elongated, pyramidal clusters cover the bush in a pale pink cloak. No fragrance. Glossy, diseaseproof leaves. Spreading, to about 3 feet tall; recommended for containers. Tolerates light shade and humidity.

The Pilgrim

English rose; 1991 / The rosettes are a delicate mass of soft, folded petals—reputedly there are 170 per blossom. The center petals are a rich yellow, fading to pale yellow or white petals at the outside. Strong, spicy scent. To 6 feet tall, more in warm climates.

The Squire

English rose; 1976 / Imbued with heady perfume second to none, the blossoms are large, velvety, and black-tinged, with a petal complexity like that of the Bourbon 'Souvenir de la Malmaison' (page 107). To about 4 feet tall. Stiff, upright habit. Susceptible to mildew.

White Meidiland

Ground cover; 1986 / The combination of dark, glossy foliage and pure white flowers gives this rose a fresh, clean look. Elongated, airy sprays of blossoms (twice the size of those of its white stablemate 'Alba Meidiland'). Faint scent. Low and spreading, to about 2 feet high and 6 feet wide.

White Pet
(Little White Pet)

Polyantha; 1879 / Clouds of little pompon blossoms appear through summer and into fall. The tiny buds are pink, and in cool weather a tint of pink may grace the open petals. Moderate to strong fragrance. Good disease resistance. To 3 feet tall, but often much smaller.

Old Garden Roses

Strictly speaking, old garden roses, also called *antique roses,* are those that existed in 1867. But many old garden rose catalogs and the listings in this section also include roses closely related to them. These wonderfully fragrant roses vary in size from giant climbers to bushes suitable for containers. Some bloom only once a year; others flower repeatedly, flush after flush, from spring until frost. (All roses listed here repeat-bloom unless noted otherwise.) Disease resistance varies among old garden roses, as does hardiness. *Rosa rugosa* is the hardiest, surviving to −35°F/−37°C or below without much protection. Most others are hardy to at least −20°F/−29°C, but China and centifolia roses generally need the same sort of winter protection hybrid teas require. Noisette and tea roses are relatively tender and best used in regions where temperatures fall no lower than about 10°F/−12°C.

In the listings, AARS means the rose has received the All-America Rose Selections award (see page 26). Alternative rose names are noted in parentheses. For an explanation of plant and flower form terms, see pages 6–7.

Alba Semi-Plena
Alba; before 1867 / The powerfully scented blossoms, each consisting of several rows of pure white petals surrounding a central clump of golden stamens, are scattered like a light snowfall over an arching, 6-foot shrub. Doesn't repeat-bloom. Red hips.

Baronne Prévost
Hybrid perpetual; 1842 / Cupped to flat, the full, bright blossoms usually have a central buttonlike eye. Heavy fragrance. Thorny stems and somewhat coarse leaves. Upright, to 6 feet tall.

Boule de Neige
Bourbon; 1867 / More than 100 richly scented, creamy white petals make up each blossom. The buds are flushed with pink, and tinges of scarlet may linger on the rounded, open blossoms. Upright form, to 5 feet.

Camaieux
Hybrid gallica; 1830 / A striking patchwork quilt of harmonious colors: white to pale pink petals show crimson and pink stripes that change to lavender and grayed purple as the flowers age. Delicious scent. Upright to arching; may reach 4 feet. Only one flush of bloom per season.

Cardinal de Richelieu
Hybrid gallica; 1847 / Round buds in small clusters open to sweetly scented, rosy violet flowers that become almost ball-shaped at maturity—by then, the shell-like petals are smoky purple with silvery reverses. Nearly thornless. Dense bush, to about 4 feet high. Tolerates humidity well. Only one burst of bloom per season.

Céline Forestier
Noisette; 1858 / The pale yellow deepens in the center, around the green button eye, and fades to cream as the blossoms age. Strongly scented. Blooms appear all summer and into fall. To 8 feet; can also be grown as a climber.

Comte de Chambord
Portland; 1860 / Upright, 3-foot plants with light green leaves produce petal-crammed, very fragrant blooms in a luscious rich pink; the flowers start out cupped, then open flat, even quartered, to reveal a button eye. Susceptible to black spot.

Crépuscule
Noisette; 1904 / The name means "twilight" in French—but this is the sun's final blaze, not the end-of-day purple shadows. Clusters of small orange buds open to sweetly fragrant blooms of bright saffron-salmon, fading to buff. Blooms all summer. A shrubby climber, to 12 feet.

Crested Moss (Cristata)
Moss; 1827 / The elaborately fringed calyx, so visible in unopened buds, accounts for the name. From this rococo cocoon emerges a typical full, cupped, spicily fragrant centifolia blossom in silvery pink. Blooms only in spring. Light green foliage. Upright, to 6 feet tall.

Ferdinand Pichard
Hybrid perpetual; 1921 / These small, striped, fragrant blossoms change color as they mature, starting pink with scarlet stripes and aging to white with purple stripes. They are usually borne in tight clusters among light green, pointed leaves. Good winter hardiness. To 6 feet tall.

Frau Karl Druschki
Hybrid perpetual; 1901 / Long, pointed buds, sometimes tinged pink, open completely even in damp regions. Lacks fragrance. Extremely vigorous, to 7 feet tall. Can be trained as a restrained climber, to about 10 feet, though a truly climbing sport is also available. Susceptible to mildew.

Dupuy Jamain
Hybrid perpetual; 1868 / Larry Parton, in Spokane, Washington, lists this rose as a favorite: "Its large, vibrant red-pink blooms are very fragrant and showy, but it doesn't get as huge as other hybrid perpetuals in my garden." To 5 feet. Good winter hardiness. For a list of Parton's recommendations, see page 123.

Great Maiden's Blush
Alba; before 1738 / This lovely, delicately scented antique has been known by various names, including *Rosa alba incarnata* and the more suggestive 'La Séduisante' and 'Cuisse de Nymphe'. Clustered, full, milky blush-pink blossoms. Plentiful foliage. To 7 feet tall and arching. Blooms once, in spring.

Henri Martin
Moss; 1862 / Lightly mossed blooms are a fragrant, rich, clear crimson, turning deep rose-pink with age. They are borne in great profusion on a 5-foot, arching plant with wiry stems and fresh green leaves. Blooms only in spring.

Henry Nevard
Hybrid perpetual; 1924 / Glowing deep crimson blossoms—large, cupped, and strongly fragrant—are perfectly complemented by ample dark foliage on a husky, upright bush, to about 5 feet tall.

Honorine de Brabant
Bourbon; date unknown / The petals are irregularly striped in purplish pink to violet, but the effect is harmonious rather than garish. Full, cupped, very fragrant blossoms are borne on a fairly tall plant, to about 6 feet, with thick foliage and few thorns. Good disease resistance.

La Ville de Bruxelles
Damask; 1849 / A prickly bush with elongated leaves bears large blooms of superb fragrance and form. Each one holds countless elaborately folded petals around a button eye. Blooms once, in spring. Upright, to about 5 feet, becoming rather spreading when freighted with blossoms.

Lady Hillingdon
Tea; 1910 / Decorative plum-purple new growth harmonizes well with the large, fragrant saffron-yellow blossoms that open from long, pointed buds. The upright, spreading bush is tall, to 6 feet, and rather open—less dense than most other teas. Often grown as a climber, to 15 feet.

Also Recommended

Anna de Diesbach (Gloire de Paris)
Hybrid perpetual; 1858 / Long, pointed buds unfurl to large, cupped clear pink blossoms that are highly fragrant. Vigorous, bushy habit; to 6 feet or taller.

Ducher
Hybrid China; 1869 / Lovely buds open to somewhat cupped, fragrant blossoms in pure white. Bronzy new leaves. To about 4 feet. Less angular than many Chinas.

Eugène de Beauharnais
Hybrid China; 1838 / Very fragrant, velvety, deep crimson blossoms appear into fall. Compact, thorny bush. Can be planted in sun or light shade. To around 3 feet tall.

Green rose (Rosa chinensis viridiflora)
Hybrid China; before 1856 / The "blossoms" are bright green sepals, not petals (see page 21). Flower arrangers are its main fans; it "flowers" through the growing season. Disease resistant. Tolerates heat. To 4 feet tall.

La Reine
Hybrid perpetual; 1842 / Very full, cupped, pink, fragrant flowers are produced in abundance on a bushy plant, to about 3 feet high.

Léda (Painted Damask)
Damask; before 1867 / Crimson markings tip the countless blush-to-white petals. Very fragrant. Blooms once, in late spring. To about 4 feet.

Lamarque

Noisette; 1830 / Plenty of pointed, medium green leaves clothe this vigorous climber. Bloom time brings a lavish display of blossoms with a powerful, sweet scent: small clusters of medium-size flowers in creamy white to palest lemon, opening from shapely buds. To 20 feet or more.

Mme. Alfred Carrière

Noisette; 1879 / It's big and vigorous, with plentiful gray-green foliage; you can use it as a climber (to 20 feet) or maintain it as a large, arching shrub (around 10 feet). The blush-white to lightest salmon-pink flowers are moderately large, full, and sweetly fragrant.

Marchesa Boccella (Marquise Boçella; Jacques Cartier)

Hybrid perpetual; 1842 / Peter Schneider, in Ohio, recommends this rose highly: "If you want to grow only one old garden rose, I recommend this one. It has all of the charm and fragrance we expect from a heritage rose without any of the drawbacks. It maintains a perfect habit, repeats continuously, has good disease resistance, and doesn't mind winter." To 4 feet tall. For a list of Schneider's recommendations, see page 122.

Mme. Hardy

Damask; 1832 / Its special beauty is in its open flowers: cupped to flat, each packed with symmetrically arranged, pristine white petals around a green center. Clusters of these fragrant blossoms decorate a moderately tall plant (to 6 feet). Blooms once, in spring.

Mme. Isaac Pereire

Bourbon; 1881 / Everything about this rose says "big"—including its intoxicating fragrance. Full-petaled blossoms of an intense purplish pink are backed by large leaves on a plant so vigorous it is better used as a small climber. Grows to 8 feet, taller as a climber. Susceptible to black spot.

Mutabilis

Hybrid China; before 1894 / Peggy Van Allen, in the Northwest, says: "My bush is four years old but not yet 3 feet tall because of winter die-back. Still, it blooms from early summer to late fall, and I love the different colors all at the same time. On the slender canes, the flowers bounce, nod, and flutter like butterflies." To 10 feet tall in warm climates; can be trained as a climber. For a list of Van Allen's recommendations, see page 123.

Reine des Violettes

Hybrid perpetual; 1860 / Intensely perfumed, full, flat flowers with a central button eye start out carmine-red, then quickly fade to shades of magenta, violet, and lavender. Nearly thornless, with gray-green leaves. To 8 feet tall.

Rêve d'Or

Noisette; 1869 / The foliage is among the best you'll see on any climbing rose—thick, semi-glossy, bronzed green. Shapely, fragrant blossoms vary from buff-apricot to gold to nearly orange, depending on the weather. Vigorous, to 18 feet; can also be grown as a very large shrub.

Rosa banksiae (Banksia rose)

Species / Where winter temperatures remain above 0°F/−18°C, these rampant climbers are smothered in pendent clusters of small blossoms in early spring. *R. b.* 'Lutea' (Lady Banks' rose) has yellow, unscented blossoms; *R. b. banksiae* (usually sold as 'Alba Plena' or 'White Banksia') has white blossoms that smell of violets. Both flower only once a season. Stems are thornless in the double forms (the single-flowered forms are rarely available). Disease-resistant foliage. Virtually evergreen in all but the coldest areas of the plant's range. Tolerates heat and humidity. Reaches 30 feet.

Rosa eglanteria (R. rubiginosa) (Sweet Brier, Eglantine)

Species / Both the flowers and the dense foliage have a green-apple scent (most pronounced in damp weather). Blooms once, in spring. Oval red to orange hips. Reaches 8 to 12 feet. Given an annual trimming, can be used as a hedge.

Rosa foetida bicolor (Austrian Copper)

Species / Few spring bloomers put on a brighter show than this rose with its blaze of coppery orange petals backed with yellow. Fragrance is strong, but some think it unpleasant. Susceptible to several foliage diseases. No repeat-bloom. From 5 to 10 feet tall.

Rosa gallica officinalis (Apothecary's Rose)

Gallica; ancient / This rose was cultivated by medieval herbalists—hence the popular name 'Apothecary's Rose'. The intensely fragrant blooms adorn a bushy, 3- to 4-foot plant with few thorns. Forms thick colonies if grown on its own roots. Doesn't repeat-bloom.

Also Recommended

Magna Charta

Hybrid perpetual; 1876 / The bright pink, cupped blossoms with hints of red are abundant, large, and fragrant. Glossy foliage. Susceptible to black spot and mildew. To 5 feet.

Maréchal Niel

Noisette; 1864 / The fragrant, soft yellow blossoms face downward. Needs a warm climate and good care. Grows 8 to 12 feet tall.

Roger Lambelin

Hybrid perpetual; 1890 / The velvety, dark, purplish red petals are precisely margined in white. Heavy fragrance. Needs regular feeding and watering. To 5 feet.

Rose du Roi à Fleurs Pourpres

Portland; 1819 / Fragrant dark red flowers have a strong infusion of purple. Bushy, to 3 feet.

Rosa gallica versicolor (Rosa mundi)

Gallica; ancient / A sport of *Rosa gallica officinalis* (page 105) and identical to it in all respects save the flowers, which are irregularly striped, dashed, and flecked pink and red on a background of white.

Rosa hugonis (R. xanthina bugonis) (Father Hugo's Rose; Golden Rose of China)

Species / In mid- to late spring, every branch is a garland of 2-inch, bright yellow blossoms with a light scent. Flowers only in spring. Pea-sized, brownish red to maroon hips. Good disease resistance. To about 8 feet tall.

Rosa moyesii

Species / A profusion of brilliant red flowers to 2½ inches across makes an arresting show. Blooms once, in spring, but in autumn bottle-shaped hips of blazing orange-red dangle from the spreading branches. Large, loose, and rather sparse; to 10 feet or so. 'Geranium' (with red flowers) and 'Sealing Wax' (with pink blooms) are shorter and more compact than the species. For areas where low temperatures in winter remain above −10°F/−23°C. Little if any scent.

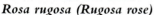

Rosa rugosa (Rugosa rose)

Species / A hybridizer could hardly have designed a rose with more virtues. Silky-petaled, fragrant flowers appear in spring, summer, and autumn. The glossy leaves have a distinctive heavy veining that gives them a crinkled appearance—and, best of all, they are nearly diseaseproof. Large "tomato" hips. From 3 to 8 feet high, spreading into colonies if grown on its own roots. Extremely tough and cold-hardy, enduring hard freezes, aridity, wind, and salt spray. Tolerant of cool summers, humidity, and heat. Excellent hedge plant. *R. r. alba* (left) has white blossoms. *R. rugosa* and *R. r. rubra* (right) have magenta-purple ones.

Rosa roxburghii (Chestnut rose, Chinquapin rose)

Species / The bud emerges from a bristly calyx that gives this disease-resistant rose its common names. Blooms once, in spring. Fragrance varies. Peeling cinnamon-colored bark on older stems. Prickly hips. To 10 feet or taller and 15 feet across. Tolerates heat and humidity.

Rosa sericea pteracantha

Species / The broad, red-brown thorns that march up the canes (see page 21) make this rose instantly recognizable. The flowers have just four petals and little or no scent; they appear once, in spring. Leaves consist of up to 19 small leaflets. Vigorous and arching, to around 10 feet.

Rose de Rescht

Portland; date unknown / These little pompons pack a powerful fragrance. Borne in clusters, they bloom continuously on a bushy, upright, 3-foot plant densely clothed in leaves. A good rose for containers.

Soleil d'Or

Hybrid foetida; 1900 / Long pointed buds unfurl to large, dusky gold, cupped blossoms that are spicy in scent. Small leaves; susceptible to black spot. To 4 feet tall.

Souvenir de la Malmaison

Bourbon; 1843 / Russ Bowermaster, in Florida, says of this rose: "It blooms early and late, with aromatic, large flowers, repeating very reliably, and it continues to bloom all winter in our climate. This is probably the most desired old garden rose for most rosarians." Reaches 4 feet. 'Kronprinzessin Viktoria' (1887) is a creamy white sport; a dark pink to rosy red sport is 'Red Souvenir de la Malmaison' (1845). For a list of Bowermaster's recommendations, see page 122.

Tuscany Superb (Superb Tuscan)

Hybrid gallica; before 1837 / Wavy petals that look as if cut from maroon velvet form a perfumed blossom with a cluster of gold stamens in the center. Few thorns. Upright, to around 4 feet. Only one flush of bloom per season.

Variegata di Bologna

Bourbon; 1909 / Cupped blossoms, in small clusters, flaunt a peppermint-stick combination of white petals striped purplish red. Fragrant. Repeat-bloom is spotty. Tall and vigorous; can be trained on a pillar or simply allowed to become a 6-foot fountain of canes. Susceptible to black spot.

Zéphirine Drouhin

Bourbon; 1868 / Richly fragrant flowers adorn the plant like a flight of butterflies. Naturally a restrained climber, from 8 to 12 feet—but treat it as a large shrub if a climber would be too large for your available space. Almost thornless. Susceptible to black spot and mildew.

Also Recommended

Souvenir du Docteur Jamain
Hybrid perpetual; 1865 / Fragrant, black-shaded petals the color of port wine compose a cupped, ruffled-looking flower. Reaches 7 feet, or 12 feet as a climber.

William Lobb (Old Velvet Moss)
Moss; 1855 / Magenta, crimson, purple, and lilac are richly mixed in the heavily mossed, strongly scented blossoms. Tall and rangy, to around 8 feet, it does best if given support or treated as a climber. No repeat-bloom.

York and Lancaster
Damask; before 1867 / The fragrant blossoms may be pinkish white, light to medium pink, or a pink-and-white combination; all variations may appear in a flower cluster. Blooms once, in late spring. Thorny. To 7 feet.

Climbing Roses

limbing roses produce long, strong canes that will grow upright on a vertical surface or freestanding structure—provided you train and tie them. They vary in size from 6 feet to 30 feet. The largest are often the ramblers; they produce massive floral displays, usually in one big flush in spring. The smallest are the pillar roses, which are just barely climbers; their canes have the desirable habit of flowering well when grown completely upright. You'll also find here climbing sports of bush roses that have long and more-or-less pliable canes. The *large-flowered climbers* (LCLs) and Kordesii climbers are natural climbers with no bush counterparts. For cold-winter regions, look for the Canadian Explorer series. All roses listed here repeat-bloom unless noted otherwise.

Choose your climbers carefully. Climbing roses take several years to reach a desirable height, and a poor choice might mean that you have to start over with a different selection.

In the listings, AARS means the rose has received the All-America Rose Selections award (see page 26). For some roses, an alternative name is noted in parentheses. For an explanation of plant and flower form terms, see pages 6–7.

Alchymist
Hybrid eglanteria; 1956 / The open blossoms have the flat, swirled and quartered form of some old garden roses and are an ever-changing mélange of gold, yellow, apricot, and pink. Glossy, bronzy green leaves. Can be a restrained climber, to 8 feet, or large shrub. Blooms only once; lovely fragrance.

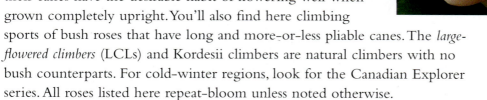

Altissimo
LCL; 1966 / Clusters of small buds open to spectacular single flowers of velvety bright red with showy yellow stamens and a light, clovelike scent. Glossy leaves add to the brilliance. Train as a small climber or pillar rose to 12 feet; or maintain as a tall shrub.

America
LCL; 1976 / This repeat-bloomer has lovely, shapely buds and large, full, highly fragrant flowers of the best hybrid tea form. Vigorous, to about 15 feet; can also be trained as a pillar rose. Susceptible to black spot. Poor winter hardiness in cold climates. AARS.

Berries 'n' Cream
LCL; 1998 / A pleasing, fruity fragrance enhances the extravagant clusters of blooms splashed with rosy pink and cream, which call to mind the ancient *Rosa gallica versicolor* (page 106). Strong 10- to 12-foot canes. Few thorns.

Blaze
LCL; 1932 / Clusters of scarlet 2- to 3-inch flowers cover the plant over a long spring bloom season. Tolerates heat well. Vigorous but not huge; ideal for fences, walls, and pillars. Slight fragrance. Susceptible to black spot and mildew. 'Blaze Improved' is reputed to repeat-flower more reliably.

Cl. Cécile Brünner (Cl. Mlle. Cécile Brünner)

Climbing polyantha; 1904 / Kathleen Brenzel, in California, says: "This climber is the star attraction in my garden, spread across three trellises to form a leafy tunnel. When its sweetheart buds open, it looks like a pink cumulus cloud." Tolerates heat. To 20 feet. Sweet scent. Healthy. May bloom till fall. The bush 'Cécile Brünner' grows to 5 feet. Not hardy in cold climates. For a list of Brenzel's recommendations, see page 124.

Cl. Iceberg

Climbing floribunda; 1968 / This is often rated the finest climbing white rose; some even call it the finest climber, period. Profuse flowering and good repeat-bloom come on a vigorous plant that reaches 15 feet. Susceptible to mildew.

Cl. Sutter's Gold

Climbing hybrid tea; 1950 / Elegant, elongated buds in classic form open to large, glowing yellow flowers, with petals warmed by a red flush. Train the 8- to 12-foot canes on a pillar or trellis. Very fragrant (the bush form won an ARS James Alexander Gamble Fragrance Medal).

Clair Matin

LCL; 1960 / Red-tinted, pointed buds open to blossoms with a cluster of gold stamens among petals of palest pink, blushing to a soft salmon hue with time. Fragrant. Consistent rebloom. Reaches 8 to 12 feet high; can also be grown as a shrub.

Compassion

LCL; 1972 / A beautiful fragrance emanates from these high-centered blooms, awash in shades of apricot, pink, and peach. Lavish rebloomer. Vigorous; climbs 9 to 15 feet; can also be kept as a shrub.

Constance Spry

Shrub/LCL; 1961 / The large, full, cupped, fragrant blossoms resemble the old European roses—and, like them, it flowers profusely in spring only. Vigorous; to 15 feet if trained as a climber but can be pruned to remain a large shrub. Disease resistant.

Also Recommended

All Ablaze

LCL; 1999 / Ruffled candy-apple-red blossoms are carried in clusters. Flowers freely through the growing season. A hint of fragrance. To 12 feet.

Blossomtime

LCL; 1951 / 'New Dawn' (page 112) is parent to this alluring climber (to 10 feet) with shell-pink blossoms that have reverses of deeper pink. Fragrant. Good bloomer. Tolerates humidity well. A shrub, or pillar rose.

Cl. Angel Face

Climbing floribunda; 1981 / Everything that makes the bush form (see page 87) so popular is available in a climber that grows to about 10 feet. Lemony scent. Poor winter hardiness in cold climates.

Don Juan

LCL; 1958 / Velvety red buds of the best hybrid tea form and size come singly or in small clusters on long stems and open well in all climates; flowers are very fragrant. A moderate climber, to about 10 feet; suitable as a pillar rose. Poor winter hardiness in cold climates.

Dortmund

Hybrid kordesii; 1955 / This rose radiates health and vigor. The blossoms are displayed against excellent foliage—holly-like and virtually disease-proof. Light to strong scent. Tolerates cool summers well. To 12 feet; much taller in warm climates. A climber, a shrub, or even a ground cover.

Dublin Bay

LCL; 1974 / This medium-size climber or pillar rose (to about 10 feet) glows with health. Velvety bright red flowers come in waves from spring into autumn. Moderate to fleeting fragrance. Foliage is plentiful and disease resistant.

Gloire de Dijon

Climbing tea; 1853 / Very full and rather flat flowers, shaped like those of its Bourbon parent, 'Souvenir de la Malmaison' (see page 107), are sweetly scented and keep coming. Susceptible to mildew, black spot, and balling. To 12 feet, but often becomes established slowly.

Fourth of July

LCL; 1999 / Kathleen Brenzel, in California, says: "Beautiful blooms in various combinations of red and white unfurl along the length of its canes, not just at the tips. Some blossoms are striped like peppermint; others are splashed or spotted with red. All have prominent yellow stamens. The effect is clean, crisp, bold." Mild scent. Tolerates heat and humidity well. To 14 feet. AARS. For a list of Brenzel's recommendations, see page 124.

Garden Sun

LCL; 1998 / This is another of Kathleen Brenzel's favorites: "In our test garden at Sunset, this lovely rose drapes over a split rail fence, bearing clusters of rich yellow blooms, with apricot blush, against deep green foliage. The fragrance is only mild, but the blooms are as cheerful as a sunny day. A neat, tailored climber with a sunny disposition." Grows 10 to 12 feet high. For a list of Brenzel's recommendations, see page 124.

Golden Showers
LCL; 1956 / Pointed buds of butter-yellow open to rather ruffled, fragrant, lighter blossoms with showy red-orange stamens. Blooms early, with an excellent fall flush. A pillar rose, but grows to 15 feet in mild climates. Susceptible to mildew. Poor winter hardiness in cold climates. AARS.

Handel
LCL; 1965 / Throughout the growing season, great numbers of shapely, hybrid tea–style buds swirl open to moderately full, creamy white flowers edged with strawberry-pink. Little fragrance. Fine bloom in fall. Susceptible to black spot. Reaches 10 to 15 feet.

Illusion
Hybrid kordesii; 1961 / Generous clusters of large, silky blossoms open scarlet-red and then turn dusky vermilion and maroon. Moderately fragrant. Blooms through the summer. Healthy foliage. Vigorous, but not big: use it on a trellis or to dress up a wall or fence.

John Cabot
Hybrid kordesii; 1978 / Clusters of fragrant flowers are borne profusely in spring, then sporadically. One of the Canadian Explorer roses, developed to withstand southern Canadian winters without protection, it makes a modest climber or a large arching shrub. Excellent disease resistance.

Joseph's Coat
LCL; 1969 / As the yellow buds expand, the color intensifies to orange; then, with exposure to sunlight, the petals flush with red, until the entire flower is crimson. To 12 feet; a climber, pillar rose, shrub, or hedge. Slight scent. Repeats now and then. Susceptible to black spot and mildew.

Lace Cascade
LCL; 1992 / From late spring onward, shapely buds open to full, ice-white flowers with a slight fragrance. Train the 10- to 12-foot canes on a pillar or trellis; or prune to a 5- to 7-foot shrub. Repeats well. Good disease resistance.

Maigold (Maygold)
Shrub; 1953 / Intensely fragrant, richly colored blooms of a bronze-gold hue appear early in the season; no rebloom. Very thorny. Tolerates humidity well. Not a large climber; encourage it to scale a pillar or spread out over a trellis; or grow it as a 5-foot shrub.

Also Recommended

Cl. Souvenir de la Malmaison
Climbing Bourbon; 1893 / Like the bush form (see page 107), but reaches 15 feet, more in mild climates. Spotty repeat-bloom. Rain may cause balling. Poor winter hardiness in cold climates.

Dynamite
LCL; 1992 / Explosions of dark red, hybrid tea–style blossoms repeat from spring into autumn on an upright pillar rose, to about 10 feet. Lightly scented. Glossy, disease-resistant foliage.

Kiftsgate
Species; 1954 / For a few weeks each summer, this giant climber (20 feet or more) glows with creamy white blossoms accented by yellow stamens. Delicious fragrance. Tolerates some shade.

Paprika
LCL; 1997 / The bright flowers of this Romantica climber-cum-shrub open in clusters, from pointed buds. Reblooms well. Slight scent. Large glossy leaves. To 10 feet.

Pierre de Ronsard (Eden)
LCL; 1987 / The plump, creamy buds and cupped, pink-blushed flowers with row upon row of petals on this Romantica rose have the style of old European roses, but they appear throughout the growing season. Slight scent. Glossy, healthy foliage. From 8 to 10 feet; a climber or pillar rose.

New Dawn
LCL; 1930 / Peter Schneider, in Ohio, says: "What repeat-blooming climber will cover an arbor in Zone 5? I know of three: 'New Dawn', 'Quadra', and 'William Baffin' [both on the next page]. But nothing beats 'New Dawn' for beauty and reliability." Bewitching scent. To about 15 feet; can be used as a pillar rose or shrub. World Rose Hall of Fame. For a list of Schneider's recommendations, see page 122.

Piñata
LCL; 1978 / Glossy foliage sets off floribunda-style, golden yellow flowers edged and washed in orange-red. An almost nonstop show of blooms. Slightly fragrant. Restrained, 8 to 10 feet, and somewhat shrubby; best used as a pillar rose or shrub.

Polka
LCL; 1996 / From plump orange buds, petals unfold and expand into large, full, fragrant, gracefully waved blossoms of golden, peachy apricot. A Romantica rose. Good for cutting. Glossy, light green leaves. To 12 feet high, or use as a shrub.

Royal Sunset
LCL; 1960 / Shapely buds of hybrid tea elegance are predominantly orange; as the flowers open, sunset tones take over, leading to buff-apricot or creamy peach with age. Fruity scent. Dark bronzy green, glossy leaves. Poor winter hardiness in cold climates. To 10 feet; a modest climber or large shrub.

Shadow Dancer
LCL; 1999 / This child of 'Dortmund' (page 110) has the same handsome, glossy, dark leaves as its parent but bigger, fancier, and more plentiful blossoms. Fragrance is only slight, but flowers appear all summer. Reaches about 8 feet, taller in mild climates.

Sombreuil

Climbing tea; 1850 / Plump buds open to flat, circular, creamy white flowers intricately packed with petals that are sometimes flushed pink and fade to white in sun. Beautifully fragrant. Reblooms sporadically. Heat tolerant. Poor winter hardiness in cold climates. To 15 feet; a climber or pillar rose.

Spectacular (*Danse du Feu*)

LCL; 1953 / Glossy, bronze foliage sets off bountiful clusters of cupped blooms shaded orange and scarlet. Fragrant. Good vigor. Grows 8 to 10 feet tall.

Rosarium Uetersen

LCL; 1977 / Russ Bowermaster, in Florida, says this about his favorite climber: "A quite large climber, with huge clusters of blooms. The first blush of bloom in the spring, following pruning, stops the traffic on the street where we live. Quite disease resistant, and repeat-blooms when spent flowers are properly pruned." Fragrant. To around 12 feet. For a list of Bowermaster's recommendations, see page 122.

Veilchenblau

Hybrid multiflora; 1909 / The most widely available of several "blue ramblers" (others are 'Violette', on this page, and 'Bleu Magenta'). Small flowers open a deep violet, sometimes streaked with white, then fade to nearly gray. Moderately fragrant. No rebloom. Grows 8 to 15 feet high.

White Dawn

LCL; 1949 / This child of 'New Dawn' (page 112) features ruffled blossoms with the scent of gardenias. Lavish spring display, moderate bloom in summer, and another big burst in fall. Good disease resistance. Tolerates humidity well. Vigorous, to about 12 feet; can be used as a climber or shrub.

William Baffin

Hybrid kordesii; 1983 / Slightly fragrant carmine-pink blossoms appear in large clusters throughout the growing season on a plant with disease-resistant foliage. One of the extra-hardy Canadian Explorer roses, it can be grown as a modest climber (to 12 feet) or a large, arching shrub.

Also Recommended

Kiss of Desire (*Harlekin*)
LCL; 1986 / Cherry-red edges the creamy white blooms. A light wild-rose scent. Repeats sporadically. Grows to 12 feet.

Quadra (*J. F. Quadra*)
Hybrid kordesii; 1981 / Pink to dark red blossoms have little if any scent. To 6 feet, more in mild climates. Hardy. Can also be used as a shrub.

Ramira (*Agatha Christie*)
LCL; 1988 / Fragrant, strawberry-pink blossoms have hybrid tea form. Reblooms well. To 12 feet, or grow as a large shrub.

Violette
Hybrid multiflora; 1921 / A "blue rambler" (see also 'Veilchenblau', left) with small, fragrant, reddish violet blooms, fading to soft mauve. Blooms once. To 15 feet.

Miniature Roses

Miniature roses are scaled-down versions of larger roses, with small leaves and smallish flowers. Most are dainty bushes—diminutive hybrid tea, shrub, or old garden roses—but some are 7-foot climbers or ground covers. Typically, miniatures bloom abundantly and almost continuously (unless otherwise stated, all the miniatures described here are repeat-bloomers). Although many are short on fragrance, there are notable exceptions. Plant them in containers or the fronts of flower beds, or use them to edge a path. They are tough plants, in the main, but, to keep them bushy and thriving, provide winter protection in regions where temperatures fall below 10°F/–12°C. Those described as short are about 1 foot high. Medium are 1 to 2 feet. Tall are over 2 feet.

In the listings, AARS means the rose has received the All-America Rose Selections award (see page 26). AoE means the rose has received the Award of Excellence from the American Rose Society, based on trials conducted for 2 years in test gardens throughout the United States. For some roses, an alternative name is noted in parentheses. For an explanation of plant and flower form terms, see pages 6–7.

Adam's Smile
1987 / Elegant, pointed buds unfurl to full blossoms with petals that roll back at the edges to create pointed petal tips. Deep pink flowers are infused with yellow on the petal backs. No scent. Glossy leaves. Medium height.

Amy Grant
1998 / Light pink, double blossoms with high centers like a hybrid tea appear singly among dark, glossy foliage. Slight fragrance. Good for cutting. Medium height.

Beauty Secret
1965 / One of the oldest miniatures and still popular, this rose produces lovely long, pointed buds that open to semidouble, cherry-red blossoms with pointed petal tips. Fragrant. Upright and bushy, to medium height. ARS Miniature Rose Hall of Fame. AoE.

Baby Love
1992 / Peter Schneider, in Ohio, says: "This is the ideal accent rose. Its neat, rounded habit makes it perfect for a container and easy to tuck into any garden space. Covered with flowers all summer long, it is one of only two roses ('Flower Carpet' [page 90] being the other) that won't black spot in my garden." Slight fragrance. Good disease resistance. Tall. For a list of Schneider's recommendations, see page 122.

Black Jade

1985 / Dusky deep red—almost black—buds of the best hybrid tea form open to full, fairly large blossoms of velvety dark red. The flowers come singly and in clusters. Little or no scent. Medium height. AoE.

Cal Poly

1991 / Brilliant color and easy care are the selling points of this rose. Against a dense backdrop of leaves, the pointed buds open to double flowers. Faint scent if any. Good disease resistance. Medium height. A climbing form (to about 8 feet) is also available. AoE.

Child's Play

1991 / The child who could color these elegant hybrid tea–style blooms would have to wield the crayons carefully: each broad white petal has a precise edging of delicate pink. Fragrant. Blooms freely. Good disease resistance. Medium height. AARS. AoE.

Crackling Fire

1999 / Coppery orange petals have deep red-orange backs. Blossoms appear in small clusters. No fragrance. Compact bush of medium height.

Cupcake

1981 / The buds and very full mature blossoms, both in a clear, cotton-candy pink, show the finest hybrid tea style. Plenty of glossy foliage completes the picture. No fragrance. Medium height. AoE.

Figurine

1991 / Borne on long stems, the long, pointed buds and full open blossoms have the smooth delicacy of fine porcelain. The petals are ivory, washed in softest pink. Fragrant. Medium height. AoE.

Also Recommended

Carnival Glass

1979 / The slightly ruffled blossoms, a blend of warm yellow, apricot, and orange, are magnificent against the glossy, bronze-tinted leaves. Bushy, medium height, spreading wider than it is tall. Good for hanging baskets.

Dreamer

1990 / Oval buds, borne either in sprays or one per stem, open to 3-inch cupped, dusty pink blossoms. Fragrance varies. Bushy, upright plant; tall.

Fairhope

1989 / The light yellow flowers, almost white on occasion, have elegant high centers and open from slender, tapered buds carried singly on long stems. Slightly fragrant. Heat tolerant. Medium height.

Giggles

1987 / An elegant combination of pinks: the deep pink buds open to blossoms of light pink with darker pink on the petal backs, and then, with age, become creamy pink. High-centered hybrid tea form. Slightly fragrant. Matte green leaves. Medium height.

Green Ice

1971 / Pink-tinted white buds open to ruffled blossoms that mature into soft pale green, sometimes with pink tinges. Little or no scent. Mounding and spreading habit. Good for hanging baskets. Medium height.

Gourmet Popcorn

1986 / Michael Ruggiero, at the New York Botanical Garden, says: "In all my 27 years of rose growing, I have not grown a better miniature rose. It produces copious numbers of 1-inch white-petaled flowers that have distinct golden stamens—the 'butter' for the popcorn. It flowers all season long until frost, whether it is deadheaded or not." Tall. For a list of Ruggiero's recommendations, see page 121.

Herbie

1987 / Rich mauve blossoms are flushed with deeper mauve at the petal edges. Shapely, like hybrid tea blossoms, they appear singly and in clusters. Slight fragrance. Bushy, to medium height.

Hot Tamale

1993 / As the shapely yellow buds unfold, the petal surfaces show a blend of orange and pink, while the undersides remain largely yellow. Blossoms are carried in small clusters. Little or no fragrance. Good disease resistance. Tall. AoE.

Irresistible

1989 / Long-stemmed, long-budded blossoms suggest a small version of the hybrid tea 'Pristine' (page 82): they are a satiny ivory-white, tinged ever so slightly with pink and centered with blush pink. Blooms profusely. Moderately fragrant. Tall.

Jean Kenneally
1984 / Elegant, pointed buds open slowly to semidouble, slightly scented flowers that are always shapely. Vigorous; blooms freely. Tolerates humidity well. Tall. AoE.

Jeanne Lajoie
1975 / This popular climbing miniature produces bountiful clusters of very double, lightly scented blossoms. Train it as a climber, from 6 to 10 feet tall; use it as a hedge; or let it develop as an arching shrub. Good disease resistance. AoE.

Lemon Gems
2000 / Deep yellow, cupped blossoms are 2½ inches across, which is large for a miniature rose. They appear mostly one per stem. Fragrance is slight. Glossy leaves. Medium height. AoE.

Lavender Jewel
1978 / The plump hybrid tea–style buds and full, fragrant 1-inch blossoms are soft lavender, tinged with magenta on the petal edges. Bushy and compact habit. Medium height.

Little Jackie
1982 / Glossy foliage provides a pleasing background for the bright combination of sherbet-orange petal surfaces and yellow petal backs. The buds are shapely, the blossoms fragrant. Medium height. AoE.

Loving Touch
1983 / Bountiful urn-shaped, apricot buds open to 3-inch, moderately double blossoms of a smooth, creamy apricot. Lightly fragrant. Spreading form. Tall. AoE.

Magic Carrousel
1972 / From bud to open bloom, you can clearly see the precise cherry-red edges to the white petals. Flowers come singly and in clusters. Little if any scent. Vigorous and free-flowering. Tall. ARS Miniature Rose Hall of Fame. AoE.

Also Recommended

Giselle
1991 / Deep pink, semidouble blossoms with paler centers are wonderfully formed and open from pointed buds. Glossy leaves. Short.

Gourmet Pheasant
1995 / Massive clusters of deep cherry-pink-to-red blossoms with golden stamens cover this fast-growing ground cover. Little scent. Glossy leaves. Medium height, to 8 feet wide.

Irish Heartbreaker
1990 / This child of 'Rise 'n' Shine', page 119, is a climber, to 5 feet tall, with Chinese-red, 2-inch, full blossoms. Slight scent.

Minilights

1987 / Abundant small yellow flowers open in clusters among glossy leaves. Spreading habit, medium height. Slight fragrance. Good disease resistance.

Minnie Pearl

1982 / Long, shapely buds of a soft ivory-infused coral-pink swirl open to full blossoms that darken a little in sunshine. Mild fragrance at best. Medium height.

Miss Flippins

1997 / Wonderfully formed, bright red blossoms with pink petal backs unfurl from long, pointed buds. The long-lasting blossoms are borne mostly singly and are good for cutting. Tolerates heat well. No fragrance. Susceptible to mildew. Tall.

Old Glory

1988 / A perfect, red, hybrid tea blossom reduced to 2½ inches across—that's 'Old Glory'. Plenty of these richly colored blossoms appear on a vigorous bush with disease-resistant foliage. Medium height. AoE.

Petite Perfection

1999 / Classy red hybrid tea–style blossoms with high centers are flushed with deep yellow at the bases of the petals and on the petal backs. Fragrance is slight, at best. Medium height.

Pierrine

1988 / Elegant pink blossoms take on apricot hues in cool weather. Most are borne one per stem; they last well and are popular for small bouquets. Mild fragrance if any. Little orange-red hips in fall. Medium height.

Popcorn

1973 / Like a popper full of corn, the full, bushy plant bursts with bloom, bearing clusters of small, globular buds and dime-sized white flowers with butter-yellow stamens. Mild fragrance. Good disease resistance. Medium height.

Pride 'n' Joy

1991 / Fat buds open to moderately full, vivid blossoms in bright orange with yellow shading on the petal backs. Fruity fragrance. Vigorous. Matte green, disease-resistant leaves. Tall. AARS.

Rainbow's End
1984 / Shapely yellow buds are touched with red on the petal tips; as the full blossoms unfold, the red appears at the petal edges (more so in sunshine, much less in shade and when skies are overcast). Little or no fragrance. Glossy leaves. Medium height. A climbing form is available; it grows from 6 to 10 feet. AoE.

Red Cascade
1976 / The name describes the effect it gives when grown in a hanging basket, but this 5-foot, lax-caned plant, with its clusters of bright red, 1-inch blossoms, can be grown as a climber, too (it's classified as a climber), or as a ground cover. AoE.

Rise 'n' Shine (Golden Sunblaze)
1977 / Beautifully shaped buds and full flowers glow like early morning sunshine on a vigorous, free-flowering bush with excellent foliage. Little or no scent. Medium height. ARS Miniature Rose Hall of Fame. AoE.

Robin Red Breast
1983 / This mini-flora (a new class of roses not quite as mini as miniatures) is an eye-catcher. The dark red, single blossoms have a white eye, and they appear among glossy, dark leaves. No fragrance. Spreading habit, medium height.

Scentsational
1995 / The first in the Scentsation series of heavily perfumed miniature roses, this mauve-pink rose has creamy pink petal backs. Good for cutting. Tall. Also in the series are 'Seattle Scentsation', a deep mauve-pink, and 'Overnight Scentsation', a medium pink.

Also Recommended

Orchid Jubilee
1992 / This climbing miniature has clusters of fluffy, pinkish lavender blossoms slightly more than an inch across. No scent. Vigorous. Let it climb, to about 6 feet, or use it as an arching shrub.

Pink Symphony (Sweet Sunblaze)
1987 / One of the Sunblaze series of miniature roses, this is a slightly fragrant, light pink double, with a center of showy yellow stamens. Leaves are dark and glossy. 'Cherry Sunblaze' is also recommended. Medium height.

Scarlet Moss
1988 / A child of 'Dortmund' (page 110) and a moss rose, this has predictably bright scarlet-red blossoms with mossy sepals. The blossoms are semidouble and borne in small sprays. Tall.

Snow Bride
1982 / Creamy buds of perfect hybrid tea form, carried both individually and in small clusters on long stems, open to pure white, moderately full, lightly fragrant blossoms. Susceptible to mildew. Medium height. AoE.

Sun Sprinkles

2001 / Deep yellow, high-centered blossoms, quite large for a miniature, are borne singly or in small clusters among glossy foliage. Light, spicy fragrance. Good disease resistance. Medium to tall. AARS. AoE.

Starina

1965 / This is a popular classic, its glossy, dark leaves framing faultless buds and blossoms that truly are hybrid teas in miniature. A little fragrance. Good disease resistance. Medium height. ARS Miniature Rose Hall of Fame.

Texas

1984 / Sunny, hybrid tea–style blooms come singly and in small clusters, borne above glossy leaves on an upright plant. Slight fragrance. Tall.

Warm Welcome

1992 / This relative of 'Cl. Sutter's Gold', page 109, is a climber, too, to 7 feet tall. The fragrant blossoms appear in small clusters. Orange-vermilion petals have yellow backs.

Winsome

1984 / Adorning a large, vigorous, dark-foliaged plant are perfect hybrid tea–form blossoms in blended tones of lilac, magenta, and purple. Slight fragrance. Tall. AoE.

Y2K

2000 / A child of 'Cal Poly', page 115, this buttery yellow hybrid tea–style rose picks up touches of red in full sun. Blossoms are slightly fragrant and borne mostly singly. Glossy leaves. Medium height.

Also Recommended

Sweet Chariot

1984 / Low and spreading when planted in the ground, it cascades gracefully when grown in a container or hanging basket. Clusters of tiny, full, grape-purple blossoms have a strong, sweet perfume. Good disease resistance. Medium height.

Top Marks

1992 / This vibrant vermilion rose has won many top European rose awards. Slightly fragrant blossoms are produced in abundance. Medium height.

Work of Art

1989 / Coral, orange, and yellow mingle in the finely formed blossoms of this climbing miniature. Slight fragrance. Stems long enough for cutting. To about 6 feet.

Regional Recommendations

Six connoisseurs of roses from different regions of the country compiled the list of roses from which we built this chapter. Here we present their recommendations by region. Michael Ruggiero made the recommendations for the Northeast; he's the senior curator of the Peggy Rockefeller Rose Garden at the New York Botanical Garden. The list for the South was drawn up by Russ Bowermaster, in Florida; he's been a rose hobbyist for 37 years and served as the American Rose Society's national chairman of judges for 6 years. Peter Schneider, who grows more than a thousand roses in Ohio and compiles the annual Combined Rose List (see page 125), made the recommendations for the Midwest. The list for the Mountain States was the work of Larry Parton, of Northland Rosarium in Spokane, Washington. Peggy Van Allen, a consulting rosarian and Skagit County, Washington, master gardener, put together the list for the Pacific Northwest. Our rose expert for California was Kathleen Brenzel, senior garden editor of *Sunset Magazine* and editor of the *Sunset Western Garden Book*.

THE NORTHEAST

PINK ROSES

Ballerina, p. 87
Betty Prior, p. 87
Buffalo Gal, p. 88
Clair Matin, p. 109
Cupcake, p. 115
Flower Carpet, p. 90
Giselle, p. 117
Jeanne Lajoie, p. 117
La Ville de Bruxelles,
    p. 103
Marchesa Boccella, p. 104
Mary Rose, p. 94
Mme. Isaac Pereire, p. 104
New Dawn, p. 112
Paris de Yves St. Laurent,
    p. 82
Pink Symphony, p. 119
Portrait, p. 83
Queen Elizabeth, p. 82
Rosarium Uetersen,
    p. 113
Sarah Van Fleet, p. 98
The Fairy, p. 100
Tiffany, p. 84
William Baffin, p. 113
Zéphirine Drouhin, p. 107

RED ROSES

Altissimo, p. 108
Black Jade, p. 115
Chrysler Imperial, p. 75
Europeana, p. 90
Hunter, p. 93
Illusion, p. 111
Ingrid Bergman, p. 78
Knock Out, p. 93
L. D. Braithwaite, p. 93
Lilli Marleen, p. 93
Mister Lincoln, p. 80
Olympiad, p. 81
Opening Night, p. 81
Precious Platinum, p. 83
Robusta, p. 97
Rosa moyesii, p. 106
Roseraie de l'Hay, p. 97

ORANGE OR WARM-BLEND ROSES

Abraham Darby, p. 86
Apricot Nectar, p. 87
Brandy, p. 74
Buff Beauty, p. 88
Caribbean, p. 75
Cary Grant, p. 75
Cl. Sutter's Gold, p. 109
Gloire de Dijon, p. 110

Livin' Easy

Glowing Peace, p. 77
Just Joey, p. 78
Livin' Easy, p. 93
Loving Touch, p. 117
Marmalade Skies, p. 94
Rêve d'Or, p. 105
Rosa foetida bicolor, p. 105
Singin' in the Rain, p. 99
Starina, p. 120
Sunset Celebration, p. 84
Tamora, p. 100

YELLOW OR CREAM ROSES

Anthony Meilland, p. 87
Cal Poly, p. 115
Gold Medal, p. 77
Golden Showers, p. 111
Golden Wings, p. 91
Graham Thomas, p. 92

Maigold, p. 111
Marco Polo, p. 79
Midas Touch, p. 80
Molineux, p. 95
Rise 'n' Shine, p. 119
Rosa banksiae 'Lutea', p. 105
Rosa hugonis, p. 106
Sunsprite, p. 99
Texas, p. 120
The Pilgrim, p. 100
Toulouse-Lautrec, p. 84

WHITE ROSES

Alba Semi-Plena, p. 101
Ducher, p. 103
Glamis Castle, p. 91
Gourmet Popcorn, p. 116
Iceberg, p. 92
Jardins de Bagatelle, p. 79
John F. Kennedy, p. 78
Mme. Alfred Carrière, p. 104
Mme. Hardy, p. 104
Pascali, p. 82
Popcorn, p. 118
Sea Foam, p. 98
Sir Thomas Lipton, p. 99
Snow Bride, p. 119
Sombreuil, p. 113
Starry Night, p. 99
White Dawn, p. 113
White Lightnin', p. 85

LAVENDER OR MAUVE ROSES

Angel Face, p. 86
Blueberry Hill, p. 88
Camaieux, p. 101
Cardinal de Richelieu,
    p. 101
Escapade, p. 89
Intrigue, p. 93
Lagerfeld, p. 79
Orchid Jubilee, p. 119
Paradise, p. 81
Reine des Violettes, p. 105
Rosa rugosa, p. 106
Rosa rugosa rubra, p. 106
Stainless Steel, p. 83
Tuscany Superb, p. 107
Veilchenblau, p. 113
William Lobb, p. 107
Winsome, p. 120

Fair Bianca, p. 90
Frau Karl Druschki, p. 102
French Lace, p. 91
Gourmet Popcorn, p. 116
Green Ice, p. 116
Irresistible, p. 116
Léda, p. 103
Margaret Merril, p. 94
Martine Guillot, p. 94
Mme. Hardy, p. 104
Pascali, p. 82
Sally Holmes, p. 97
Snow Owl, p. 99
White Lightnin', p. 85

LAVENDER ROSES
Cardinal de Richelieu, p. 101
Cardinal Hume, p. 88
Eugène de Beauharnais, p. 103
Florence Delattre, p. 91
Heirloom, p. 78
Herbie, p. 116
Lagerfeld, p. 79
Moon Shadow, p. 81
Paradise, p. 81
Reine des Violettes, p. 105
Sweet Chariot, p. 120
Veilchenblau, p. 113
Violette, p. 113
Winsome, p. 120

MULTICOLOR ROSES
Carefree Delight, p. 88
Child's Play, p. 115
Dortmund, p. 110
Double Delight, p. 76
Fourth of July, p. 110
Hot Tamale, p. 116
Love, p. 79
Oranges 'n' Lemons, p. 95
Pierre de Ronsard, p. 112
Pink Meidiland, p. 96
Rainbow's End, p. 119
Robin Red Breast, p. 119
Roger Lambelin, p. 105
Rosa gallica versicolor, p. 106
Warm Welcome, p. 120

THE MOUNTAIN STATES

PINK ROSES
Anna de Diesbach, p. 103
Aunt Honey, p. 86
Bonica, p. 88
Conrad Ferdinand Meyer, p. 89
Country Dancer, p. 89
Earth Song, p. 76
Gourmet Pheasant, p. 117
Guy de Maupassant, p. 91
Jeanne Lajoie, p. 117
Johann Strauss, p. 93
Magna Charta, p. 105
New Dawn, p. 112
Paris de Yves St. Laurent, p. 82
Pink Peace, p. 82
Sevilliana, p. 99
The Fairy, p. 100
Tiffany, p. 84
Tournament of Roses, p. 84
Zéphirine Drouhin, p. 107

RED ROSES
All Ablaze, p. 109
Altissimo, p. 108
Dublin Bay, p. 110
Dupuy Jamain, p. 102
Henry Nevard, p. 103
Knock Out, p. 93
L. D. Braithwaite, p. 93
Loving Memory, p. 79
Mister Lincoln, p. 80
Oklahoma, p. 81
Olympiad, p. 81
Opening Night, p. 81
Queen Bee, p. 97
Rouge Royal, p. 83
Scarlet Meidiland, p. 97
Traviata, p. 85
Uncle Joe, p. 85

ORANGE OR WARM-BLEND ROSES
Abbaye de Cluny, p. 74
Chris Evert, p. 75
Easy Going, p. 90
Garden Sun, p. 110

Lasting Peace, p. 79
Livin' Easy, p. 93
Marie Curie, p. 94
Marmalade Skies, p. 94
Octoberfest, p. 81
Polka, p. 112
Solitude, p. 83
Tamora, p. 100
Touch of Class, p. 85

YELLOW OR CREAM ROSES
Anthony Meilland, p. 87
Arthur Bell, p. 89
Elina, p. 77
Gold Medal, p. 77
Heart O' Gold, p. 77
Mellow Yellow, p. 81
Michelangelo, p. 80
Sunsprite, p. 99

WHITE ROSES
Boule de Neige, p. 101
Frau Karl Druschki, p. 102
Honor, p. 78
Iceberg, p. 92
John F. Kennedy, p. 78
Moonstone, p. 80
Sally Holmes, p. 97
Starry Night, p. 99
White Dawn, p. 113
White Lightnin', p. 85

LAVENDER OR MAUVE ROSES
Moje Hammarberg, p. 95
Outta the Blue, p. 95
Rose du Roi à Fleurs Pourpres, p. 105
Scabrosa, p. 99

MULTICOLOR ROSES
Carefree Wonder, p. 89
Desert Peace, p. 76
Dortmund, p. 110
Double Delight, p. 76
Ferdinand Pichard, p. 102
Handel, p. 111
Honorine de Brabant, p. 103
Mikado, p. 81
Mountain Music, p. 95
Paprika, p. 112
Piccadilly, p. 81

Sexy Rexy

Pink Meidiland, p. 96
Playboy, p. 96
Prairie Sunset, p. 96
Regensburg, p. 97
Spectacular, p. 113

THE PACIFIC NORTHWEST

PINK ROSES
Ballerina, p. 87
Bonica, p. 88
Cécile Brünner, p. 109
China Doll, p. 89
Crested Moss, p. 102
Dainty Bess, p. 76
Fame! p. 76
Flower Carpet, p. 90
Jeanne Lajoie, p. 117
Mme. Isaac Pereire, p. 104
New Zealand, p. 81
Queen Elizabeth, p. 82
Rosa eglanteria, p. 105
Rosa gallica officinalis, p. 105
Rosa roxburghii, p. 106
Sexy Rexy, p. 98
Souvenir de la Malmaison, p. 107
The Fairy, p. 100
Tiffany, p. 84
Tournament of Roses, p. 84

RED ROSES
Altissimo, p. 108
Dr. Jackson, p. 89
Hansa, p. 92
Ingrid Bergman, p. 78
Irish Heartbreaker, p. 117
Olympiad, p. 81
Opening Night, p. 81
Red Ribbons, p. 97

Double Delight

Resources and Suppliers

INFORMATION RESOURCES

American Rose Society
P.O. Box 30,000
Shreveport, LA 71130-0030
(318) 938-5402
www.ars.org
*The ARS offers rose gardeners
an extensive array of information and services, including
regional evaluations of rose varieties and advice from local ARS
experts. Contact the society to
learn about membership.*

The Combined Rose List
Peter Schneider
P.O. Box 677
Mantua, OH 44255
www.combined roselist.com
*The ultimate shopping guide,
updated annually, this booklet
provides an index of all roses
commercially available.*

MAIL-ORDER SUPPLIERS

The widest variety of roses
is available by mail order.

MODERN ROSES
Edmunds' Roses
6235 S.W. Kahle Road
Wilsonville, OR 97070-
    9727
(503) 682-1476
(888) 481-7673
www.edmundsroses.com

Jackson & Perkins Company
One Rose Lane
Medford, OR 97501
(800) 292-4769
www.jacksonandperkins.com

Tate Nursery
10306 FM Road 2767
Tyler, TX 75708-9239
(903) 593-1020
www.tyler-roses.com

MODERN AND OLD GARDEN ROSES
The Antique Rose
    Emporium
9300 Lueckemeyer Road
Brenham, TX 77833-6453
(800) 441-0002
www.weAREroses.com

Arena Roses
525 Pine Street
P.O. Box 3570
Paso Robles, CA 93447
(805) 238-3742
(888) 466-7434
www.arenaroses.com

Heirloom Roses
24062 Riverside Drive N.E.
St. Paul, OR 97137
(503) 538-1576
www.heirloomroses.com

Heritage Roses of
    Tanglewood Farm
16831 Mitchell Creek Drive
Fort Bragg, CA 95437-8727
(707) 964-3748

High Country Roses
P.O. Box 148
Jensen, UT 84035
(800) 552-2082
www.highcountryroses.com

Hortico, Inc.
723 Robson Road R.R. 1
Waterdown, Ontario
    L0R 2H1
Canada
(905) 689-6984
www.hortico.com

Mt. Hood

Martin & Kraus
1191 Centre Road
P.O. Box 12
Carlisle, Ontario L0R 1H0
Canada
(905) 689-0230
www.gardenrose.com

Mendocino Heirloom Roses
P.O. Box 904
Redwood Valley, CA 95470
(707) 485-6219
www.heritageroses.com

Muncy's Rose Emporium
11207 Celestine Pass
Sarasota, FL 34240
(941) 377-6156
www.muncyrose.com

Northland Rosarium
9405 S. Williams Lane
Spokane, WA 99224
(509) 448-4968
www.northlandrosarium.com

Petaluma Rose Company
P.O. Box 750953
Petaluma, CA 94975
(707) 769-8862
www.petrose.com

Pickering Nurseries, Inc.
670 Kingston Road
Pickering, Ontario L1V 1A6
Canada
(905) 839-2111
www.pickeringnurseries.com

Regan Nursery
4268 Decoto Road
Fremont, CA 94555
(510) 797-3222
(800) 249-4680
www. regannursery.com

Spring Valley Roses
P.O. Box 7
Spring Valley, WI 54767
(715) 778-4481
www.springvalleyroses.com

Petite Perfection

Vintage Gardens
2833 Old Gravenstein
    Highway South
Sebastopol, CA 95472
(707) 829-2035
www.vintagegardens.com

Wayside Gardens
1 Garden Lane
Hodges, SC 29695-0001
(800) 845-1124
www.waysidegardens.com

MINIATURE ROSES
Justice Miniature Roses
5947 S.W. Kahle Road
Wilsonville, OR 97070
(866) 836-8840
www.justiceminiature
    roses.com

Michigan Miniature Roses
45951 Hull Road
Belleville, MI 48111
(734) 699-6698
www.michiganmini
    roses.com

Nor'East Miniature Roses
P.O. Box 307
Rowley, MA 01969
(800) 426-6485
www.noreast-miniroses.com

Tiny Petals Nursery
2880 Ramsey Cut-Off
Silver Springs, NV 89429
(775) 577-4474
www.tinypetalsnursery.com

Subject Index

Pages listed in *italics* include photographs.

Great Maiden's Blush

Plant Index

Pages listed in *italics* include photographs.

Abbaye de Cluny, *6, 74*
Abraham Darby, 19, *86*
Adam's Smile, *114*
Agatha Christie (Ramira), 113
Alba Meidiland, 100
Alba Plena *(Rosa banksiae banksiae), 105*
Alba Semi-Plena, *101*
Alberic Barbier, 29, *65, 69*
Alchymist, *108*
All Ablaze, 109
All That Jazz, *86*
Altissimo, 29, *108*
America, *14, 108*
Amy Grant, *114*
Angel Face, 87
Anna de Diesbach, 103
Anthony Meilland, 87
Apothecary's Rose *(Rosa gallica officinalis), 105*
Apricot Nectar, 87
Artemisia 'Powis Castle', *17*
Arthur Bell, 29, *89*
Artistry, *74*
Astilbe, *11*
Aunt Honey, *86*
Austrian Copper *(Rosa foetida bicolor), 105*
Autumn Sunset, 87

Baby Love, 9, *114*
Ballerina, 29, *87*
Banksia rose *(Rosa banksiae), 105*
Barberry *(Berberis), 13*
Baronne Prévost, *101*
Beauty Secret, *114*
Belle Story, *19, 87*
Berberis (barberry) *13*
Berries 'n' Cream, *108*
Betty Boop, *87*
Betty Prior, 29, *87*
Bewitched, 44, *74*
Black Jade, *115*
Blanc Double de Coubert, *88*
Blaze, 15, *28, 29, 108*
Blossomtime, 29, 109
Blueberry Hill, *88*
Blue elymus grass, *9*
Bonica, 16, *17, 88*
Boule de Neige, *101*
Boxwood *(Buxus), 12*
Brandy, 44, *74*
Bride's Dream, 13, 44, *75*
Brigadoon, *75*
Buffalo Gal, 21, *88*
Buff Beauty, 29, *88*
Buxus (Boxwood), *12*

Cal Poly, *115,* 120
Camaieux, *101*
Candelabra, *75*
Cardinal de Richelieu, 29, *101*
Cardinal Hume, *88*
Carefree Delight, 16, *88*

Carefree Wonder, 16, *89*
Caribbean, *75*
Carnival Glass, 115
Cary Grant, *75*
Catmint *(Nepeta), 8, 10, 17*
Céline Forester, *102*
Champlain, *89*
Charlotte, 89
Cherokee rose *(Rosa laevigata), 21*
Cherry Sunblaze, 119
Chestnut rose *(Rosa roxburghii), 21, 106*
Child's Play, *115*
China Doll, 9, *89*
Chinquapin rose *(Rosa roxburghii), 106*
Chris Evert, 75
Chrysler Imperial, *19, 75*
Cl. Angel Face, 109
Cl. Cécile Brünner, *14, 29, 109*
Cl. Iceberg, *109*
Cl. Souvenir de la Malmaison, 111
Cl. Sutter's Gold, *109,* 120
Clair Matin, 15, *109*
Claridge Druce (geranium), *21*
Clematis 'Elsa Spath', *67*
Clematis florida sieboldii, 18
Columbine, *45*
Compassion, *109*
Complicata, *63*
Comte de Chambord, *102*
Conrad Ferdinand Meyer, 16, 19, 89
Constance Spry, *109*
Coral Dawn, *56–57*
Country Dancer, *89*
Crackling Fire, *115*
Crépuscule, *102*
Crested Moss, 19, 20, *102*
Crimson Bouquet, *75*
Crimson Glory, 19, *75*
Crystalline, 44, *76*
Cuisse de Nymphe, *103*
Cupcake, 9, *115*

Dainty Bess, *19, 76*
Danse du Feu (Spectacular), *113*
Daylily *(Hemerocallis), 17*
Delicata, *6, 89*
Desert Peace, *76*
Diascias, *8*
Distant Drums, *89*
Don Juan, *110*
Dortmund, *15, 29, 110, 112,* 119
Double Delight, *19,* 44, *76, 124*
Dr. Huey, *26*
Dr. Jackson, 21, *89*
Dreamer, 115
Dublin, 13, *19, 76*
Dublin Bay, *110*

Ducher, 103
Dupuy Jamain, 19, *102*
Dynamite, 111

Earth Song, *76, 86*
Easy Going, *90*
Eden (Pierre de Ronsard), *112*
Eglantine *(Rosa eglanteria), 105*
Elina, 13, 44, 77
Elsa Spath (clematis), *67*
Elymus grass, *9*
Escapade, 16, *89*
Eugène de Beauharnais, 29, 103
Euphorbia, *10, 11*
Europeana, 29, *90*

Fair Bianca, *90*
Fairhope, 29, *115*
Fame! 44, *76*
Father Hugo's Rose *(Rosa hugonis), 106*
Ferdinand Pichard, *102*
Figurine, *115*
Fire Meideland, 91
First Light, *90*
Florence Delattre, *91*
Flower Carpet, 9, *17, 17,* 29, *90,* 114
Flutterbye, *91*
Folklore, *77*
Fourth of July, 15, 29, *110*
Fragrant Cloud, 13, 19, 44, 77
Frau Karl Druschki, *102*
French Lace, 9, *91*

Garden Sun, 15, *110*
Gemini, 13, *77*
Geranium *(Rosa moyessii),* 106
Geranium, species, *10*
Gertrude Jekyll, *13*
Giggles, *116*
Gingersnap, 91
Giselle, 117
Glamis Castle, *91*
Gloire de Dijon, *110*
Gloire de Paris (Anna de Diesbach), 103
Glowing Peace, *77*
Golden Celebration, *91,* 95
Golden Rose of China *(Rosa hugonis), 106*
Golden Showers, *18, 111*
Golden Sunblaze (Rise 'n' Shine), *119*
Golden Wings, 29, *91*
Gold Medal, 29, 44, *77*
Gourmet Pheasant, 17, *117*
Gourmet Popcorn, 9, 29, *116*
Graham Thomas, *92,* 95
Great Maiden's Blush, *103, 126*
Green Ice, *116*
Green rose *(Rosa chinensis viridiflora),* 21, 29, 103
Guy de Maupassant, *91*

Handel, 15, *111*
Hansa, 16, 21, *92*
Harlekin (Kiss of Desire), 113
Hawkeye Belle, *9*
Heart O' Gold, *77*

Robin Red Breast

Heidelberg, *92*
Heirloom, *78*
Hemerocallis (daylily), *17*
Henri Martin, 20, *103*
Henry Nevard, *103*
Herbie, *116*
Himalayan poppy *(Meconopsis), 11*
Honor, 44, *78*
Honorine de Brabant, *103*
Hot Tamale, *116*
Hunter, 29, *93*
Hydrangea, *45*

Iceberg, *8, 10,* 16, *17,* 29, *92*
Illusion, *111*
Imperata (Japanese blood grass), *9*
Ingrid Bergman, 13, 29, *78*
Intrigue, 19, 29, *93*
Iris, *9*
Irish Heartbreaker, 117
Irresistible, *116*
Ispahan, *18*

Jacques Cartier (Marchesa Boccella), *104*
Japanese blood grass *(Imperata), 9*
Jardins de Bagatelle, 13, *19, 79*
Jean Kenneally, 29, *117*
Jeanne Lajoie, 15, *117*
Johann Strauss, 93
John Cabot, *111*
John F. Kennedy, *78*
Joseph's Coat, *71, 111*
Joyfulness, *78*
Jupiter's beard, *45*
Just Joey, *28,* 29, 44, *78*

Kaleidoscope, *92*
Kathleen, 21, 29, *92*
Kiftsgate, 19, 29, 111
King's Ransom, *78*
Kiss of Desire, 113
Knock Out, 16, 21, 29, *93*
Kordes' Perfecta, 29, *78*
Kronprinzessin Viktoria, 107

L. D. Braithwaite, *93*
Lace Cascade, *111*
Lady Banks' rose *(Rosa banksiae), 105*
Lady Hillingdon, *103*
Lady X, *79*
Lagerfeld, 44, *79*
Lamarque, *16, 104*
La Reine, 103
La Séduisante, *103*
Lasting Peace, *79*

Soleil d'Or